HOW TO PAINT
CITADEL
MINIATURES

CONTENTS

By
Rick Priestley

Production:
Dylan Owen,
John Michelbach, Adam Shaw

Illustrations: Nuala Kennedy

Stages Painted by:
Dave Andrews, Kev Asprey,
John Cadice, Nik Cristofoli,
Dave Cross, David Imrie,
Tammy Haye, Ben Jefferson,
Rick Priestley, Joe Sleboda,
Dave Taylor & Ted Williams.

Additional Painting:
Keith Robertson, Kev Asprey,
Kevin Dallimore, Mark Jones, Seb Perbet,
Kirsten Mickelburgh & Simon Tift.

Thanks to Dave Cross & John Blanche.
Orc image on page 38 courtesy
of Climax and Warhammer Online.

PRODUCED BY GAMES WORKSHOP

Games Workshop, the Games Workshop logo, Citadel and the Citadel Castle, Warhammer, 'Eavy Metal and all associated marks, logos, devices, names, characters, illustrations and images from the Warhammer and Warhammer 40,000 universes are either ®, TM and/or © Games Workshop Ltd., 2000-2003, where applicable registered in the UK and other countries around the world. All Rights Reserved.

The Lord of The Rings © 2003 New Line Productions, Inc. The Lord of The Rings and the characters,names and places therein, TM The Saul Zaentz Company d/b/a Tolkien Enterprises under license to New Line Productions, Inc. All Rights Reserved.

British cataloguing-in-Publication Data. A catalogue record for this book is available from the British Library.

UK	US	Australia	Canada	Japan
Games Workshop, Willow Rd, Lenton, Nottingham, NG7 2WS	Games Workshop, 6721 Baymeadow Drive, Glen Burnie, Maryland, 21060-6401	Games Workshop, 23 Liverpool Street, Ingleburn, NSW 2565	2679 Bristol Circle, Units 2&3, Oakville, Ontario, L6H 6Z8	Games Workshop, Willow Rd, Lenton, Nottingham, NG7 2WS, UK

NEW LINE CINEMA
An AOL Time Warner Company

Lord of the Rings website:
www.lordoftherings.net

AMERICA
Online

AOL keyword:
Lord of the Rings

ISBN: 1-84154-366-7   Games Workshop website: www.games-workshop.com   Product Code: 60 04 99 99 072

PREFACE

How to Paint Citadel Miniatures is an introduction and general guide to assembling and painting Citadel miniatures, whether plastic or metal. The chosen examples concentrate on the most popular Games Workshop ranges, namely models for Warhammer, Warhammer 40,000, and The Lord of The Rings – but the methods and materials discussed are applicable to all similar models.

This book is for everyone who wants to learn more about painting miniatures, whether for wargames or display. It has been produced with the collector of armies in mind but it covers a whole range of techniques from the basic to the most complex. All techniques are explained and shown in clear close-up photographs or line drawings. The working methods of individual painters are presented in a series of detailed stage by stage photographs with accompanying hints and tips. The overall aim of this guide has been to show a variety of styles to suit different tastes and stimulate experimentation rather than championing any particular 'look' or technique.

Converting miniatures and the art of modelling has not been covered beyond the process of basic assembly. Similarly, tank and vehicle painting was felt to be a complex subject in its own right and has been covered only in the most general way. Dioramas, scratch building, figure sculpting and constructing and painting scenery have been cheerfully ignored. All would undoubtedly make excellent subjects for the experienced painter but lie beyond the scope of this title – rather than tackle these in a half-hearted way they have been left for future volumes and more expert authors.

Whatever your chosen subjects, level of skill, or personal ambitions, I hope you find this guide both informative and entertaining. Its contents reflects the efforts and undeniable talents of some of the most accomplished miniatures artists working today, to all of whom I would like to extend my thanks for their inspiring contributions. Finally, whether you are starting your first collection or are a veteran with many worn-out brushes to your credit, I can only wish that you continue to enjoy painting, developing your talents and watching your armies grow far into the future.

Rick P

Rick Priestley
Nottingham, 2003

MATERIALS

The first thing you will need is a place where you can paint comfortably. It is important not to underestimate the effect this will have on your work. If you create an environment that is relaxing, you will look forward to your painting sessions as a chance to get away from everyday drudgery. Give yourself some space and you will be able to work longer and more effectively too. So, start by making some room for painting, preferably well away from the family or TV, in your own room or den where you won't be disturbed.

You will need a reasonably sized flat surface, such as a table or desk, positioned as closely to a window as possible to provide plenty of natural daylight. We'll come to the matter of artificial lighting in due course, but for now let it be said that there is nothing as good as natural light when it comes to distinguishing colour and detail – so take advantage of it when you can.

Your tabletop is going to take quite a battering by the time you have finished drilling, sawing, filing and gluing, let alone spilling paint, water

and tea, so it's essential to lay down a good, thick layer of newspaper.

If you have a desk that can be dedicated to painting then it is a good idea to fasten a thick piece of corrugated cardboard over the whole surface and lay the newspaper onto that – this makes an excellent protective layer. If you are obliged to use a family table then take extra care – in this case it is best to lay a separate sheet of board over the table with a thick pad of newspaper between the table and board. Don't kid yourself that you won't spill things… you will… so make sure that any potential disaster is safely contained.

Whilst on the subject of house and home, it's virtually impossible to remove paint from carpets or other fabrics, including clothes. So, wear suitable clothes and not your Sunday best! If a carpet is involved, it's a good idea to put an old rug over it before you begin to paint. Better still, use a piece of synthetic floor covering that won't absorb spilled paint and can be easily cleaned.

TOOLS OF THE TRADE

There is no need to buy everything at once. Most of us build up a collection of tools and paints over a few years. Paints and brushes are obviously essential right from the start, but some tools are only needed occasionally or for specialist jobs, and can be purchased as and when needed.

Brushes

You will need a minimum of two brushes: one small brush for detail and a larger brush for painting bases and bigger areas – the Citadel Detail and Standard size brushes are ideal. Replace your brushes as they lose their points – old brushes can be kept for tough work such as applying glue, stirring paint, or painting rough surfaces such as textured bases.

If you intend to paint larger models it's worth investing in a much larger brush right away, such as a Citadel Base Coat or Large size brush. The smallest sized brushes, such as the Citadel Fine Detail brush, are handy for painting into hard-to-reach recesses but don't have finer points than larger brushes and aren't essential.

Dry Brushes

These are brushes with hard-wearing bristles that are designed to be used in conjunction with the drybrushing technique described later in this book. Any brush can be used with a 'dry' technique but ordinary brushes will quickly lose their points and become useless for other work.

Taking care of brushes

Good brushes are essential for the sort of fine, detailed work that we shall be undertaking – unfortunately they are also expensive. Look after your brushes and not only will they last longer but you'll find that they are far easier to use. So, rule number one, at the end of every session clean all your brushes in cold, clean water, using a little soap if necessary, repoint them between thumb and forefinger, and store them carefully so that the points don't get damaged. Don't use hot water to clean brushes as this may unseat the bristles. Many people keep their brushes point uppermost in an old mug or jar, which protects the tips and looks very arty.

It is also important to take care of your brushes as you paint. Avoid getting so much paint onto the brush that it cakes around where the bristles join the metal ferrule. This will ruin a brush very quickly. It is best not to stir paint with a good brush for the same reason. If you need to stir, use an old brush, a brush handle, cocktail stick, or something similar.

Time to buy a new brush!
Once a brush won't easily make a good point, it can be used for back-up duties such as drybrushing, applying glue and stirring paint.

Water Pot

An old mug or jar makes an ideal water pot. Clean water is used to thin paint and to clean brushes. It's a good habit to start each session with clean water and to change the water for fresh when it becomes dirty.

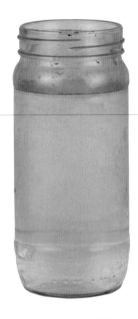

Wipes

For drying brushes, wiping away paint, and blowing your nose – any tissue or soft kitchen paper will suffice. Some people prefer a clean rag.

Palette

If you want to mix or thin paint then you will need a palette and the best thing to use is a large, white plate – but a saucer, tile, or a proper art palette will do the job too.

Whatever you use will become encrusted with paint during each session – if you let this build up it will become dirty and almost impossible to shift. The ideal practice is to clean your palette in hot soapy water once you have cleaned your brushes at the end of each session. If you let the paint dry, the easiest way to shift it is to soak the palette in hot water so that the paint becomes soft and then use a scouring pad to remove it.

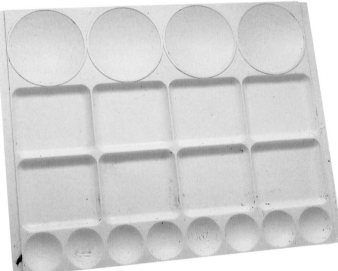

Desk Lamp

For painting in the evening you'll need a good desk lamp fitted with a colour adjusted 'daylight' bulb. An ordinary bulb will illuminate your work area perfectly satisfactorily but colours will often look very different under artificial light compared to daylight.

Of course, if your models are only going to be seen under artificial light then this may not be a problem! A daylight bulb mimics daylight and can be obtained from shops that sell art and craft materials.

Clippers

Although you can get away without buying a pair of clippers straightaway, you'll find the expenditure worthwhile. Clippers are useful for removing plastic pieces from their sprue and separating small castings from their metal tags – metal pieces, no matter their thickness, are generally too hard to cut any thickness safely with a knife, so clippers are needed if you want to modify or convert your models.

Drill or Pin-Vice

You will need one of these if you want to drill holes in either metal or plastic. This is only likely to be necessary if you are undertaking a substantial conversion or modelling project, but some large winged models must be 'drilled and pinned' if they are to stand much handling.

Glue

You will need superglue to assemble metal models, polystyrene cement or liquid 'poly' for assembling plastic components, and PVA (woodwork) glue for applying base material such as sand, Static Grass, or flock as described later.

Pliers

These are useful for bending pieces into position and fixing wire 'pins' when assembling larger models.

Craft Knife

Recent governmental legislation in some over-regulated parts of the world has made it increasingly difficult to obtain good craft knives, but nonetheless you are going to need one. If you buy one tool, make it a good knife – it will be necessary for cleaning up castings prior to assembly and removing small parts from plastic frames. It is also worth buying a proper cutting mat to use with the knife so that you can avoid cutting directly onto your work surface.

Tweezers

For handling small components and applying transfers – handy if you intend to make a lot of plastic kits.

Files

After a knife, a set of files is the most useful part of your tool kit – used for cleaning and smoothing castings and filing pieces 'to fit' where necessary. Files come in different profiles – flat, round, half-round, etc, and it is a good idea to have a selection.

Base Material

Sand, flock, small pebbles or Static Grass makes the ideal material for finishing bases – we'll discuss the merits of each later (see page 58).

Jeweller's Saw

This is a very fine-toothed saw with an extremely delicate blade that is used to make fine cuts in metal.

You won't need one of these unless you are intending to convert models by cutting and swapping components – a specialist tool for experienced modellers.

IMPORTANT!

If you share your house with young children or pets, knives, saws and other modelling tools must be put out of harm's way at the end of each session.

Junior Hacksaw

A brutal and cheap household tool for cutting large pieces of metal. You really won't need a hacksaw unless you are making substantial modifications to large models or scenic items, or fixing your plumbing!

Sculpting Tool and Putty

This is the same tool and the same putty that the Citadel Design teams use to make our models. If you're up to the job, these can be used to remodel features or make your own models from scratch. The putty is also very good for filling gaps in larger multi-piece models. It is very tough once set and can also be used to attach pieces in some situations – for example, fixing riders onto horses.

Plasticine, tape, wire, elastic bands

These are useful odds and ends. Plasticine, Blu-tack or any similar soft adhesive putty is useful for holding components whilst they dry – elastic bands and tape are useful for holding together larger components. Wire (either brass rod or soft wire) is needed to make metal pins to hold larger metal components together. Plasticine, or any similar soft modelling clay, is useful for filling gaps in areas that won't be handled much.

Paint

The Citadel Colour paint range provides a complete and exhaustive breadth of colours and has been formulated especially for painting metal models. The paint is water based but waterproof once dry. It is fully intermixable with other acrylic artists' paints should you wish to do so.

The colours you will need depend very much on the subjects you are going to paint – but a good starter selection consists of the following:

Chaos Black; Skull White; Enchanted Blue; Sunburst Yellow; Blood Red; Goblin Green; Bestial Brown; Mithril Silver.

With these basic colours it is possible to paint pretty much anything by mixing the colours together. If your budget will stretch to it, buy a strong green and blue as well (Dark Angels Green and Regal Blue, for example).

The next most useful colours are a variety of browns as these are difficult to mix (Snakebite Leather, Scorched Brown, and Vermin Brown are a good yellow, dark, and red brown respectively – Bestial Brown is a mid-shade). Shining Gold is the most useful metallic paint after Mithril Silver. Most of the other shades can be mixed from those already mentioned, but it is worth getting specific colours if you are intending to use them a great deal as this saves mixing and ensures that the colours are consistent. Many people find flesh tones hard to mix, so if you are painting humans or other flesh coloured creatures, invest in an appropriate base colour.

Ink and Varnish

The Citadel Colour range also includes transparent inks and varnish. These are useful for specific techniques as we shall see later – make it a priority to buy the paint you need first. The most useful of the inks are the strong and dark colours such as red, blue, yellow, black, and brown.

Spray Paint

You'll need a can of white or black undercoat depending on your subject and chosen style. You can also paint vehicles and similar large models with an overall coat of spray paint to provide a coloured base for further work. Although it is not strictly speaking necessary to apply a spray undercoat, it is necessary to use some kind of undercoat – and a spray provides the best 'key' between the model and top layer of paint.

Paint Station

This is part of the Citadel Modelling range, but a similar effect can be achieved with a tray or small sheet of board. Basically, it's a mobile painting desk that you can move about as required – very useful if you don't have a permanent set-up or if you just fancy painting in front of the telly. This one has cut-outs to hold a water container and brushes, and handles to make it easy to move about.

PREPARATION

No matter what models you intend to paint you will need to begin by cleaning up the metal castings or plastic mouldings, gluing the components together, and applying an undercoat before the models are ready to begin painting.

If you are putting together a whole Warhammer regiment or Warhammer 40,000 squad then it's best to prepare all the models and get them ready for painting at the same time. This makes the process much quicker than assembling and painting the models one at a time. Painting the whole unit at once also makes it easier to finish the models in consistent colours.

Some people like to assemble and paint a single example first as a 'test piece' before finishing the rest of a unit. This obviously takes a little longer, but it's a good idea if you're uncertain about your chosen scheme. Should you dislike the result, it is far better to have one model to repaint than a whole regiment.

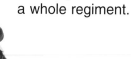

Space Marines

ASSEMBLING METAL MODELS

Take the pieces from their packaging and make sure that they are all present and correct. Metal models often consist of several metal parts, usually have a separate plastic base and can include other plastic parts too.

Before assembling the pieces, check each metal casting for minor imperfections such as mould lines, vent marks and flashing.

These are the result of the casting process and unavoidable to some degree, but all can be easily dealt with.

MOULD LINES

Metal pieces are produced from rubber moulds that consist of two halves – if you look closely you may be able to see a faint mould line running all the way around the model where the two mould halves join. If the line is pronounced enough to be felt with your thumbnail it will probably show once the model is painted.

A few moments' work will quickly remove visible mould lines. Take either a knife or file and carefully scrape or file away the line. Pay particular attention on highly visible smooth surfaces, such as Space Marine shoulder pads or armoured panels.

Don't worry too much if lines pass over highly textured surfaces such as hair or fur, as these won't be nearly as obvious once the model is finished.

The models on this page have been stained for photographic purposes

VENTS

Vents are thin channels cut or drilled into the rubber moulds to allow air to escape. This procedure ensures that air is expelled from the mould as it fills.

Sometimes the vents themselves fill with metal, producing a little strand or a small scar where the vent touches the casting. On the whole this is a good sign as it means the mould has filled completely. It is usually very easy to remove these little strands with your thumbnail. Where vent marks leave tiny 'blip' scars, use your file to file them flat.

FLASHING

Flashing sometimes occurs where hot metal runs between the two mould halves producing a thin layer of unwanted metal, often between a model's legs. This is not a problem as the layer is very thin, rather like foil, and can easily be removed using a knife, with any resultant mould line filed smooth.

Flashing is more common with large castings where the volume of molten metal is more likely to force its way 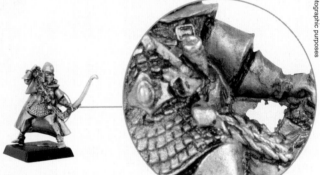 *between the mould halves, but it is easily removed if it has not already detached itself during manufacturing.*

The models on this page have been stained for photographic purposes

Once you have cleaned up the metal pieces do the same for any plastic components (as described later) and test the pieces for fit. Metal pieces may not fit exactly perfectly, and the larger the pieces are, the more inexact the fit is likely to be, so it is important to make sure the fit is adequate before gluing anything together.

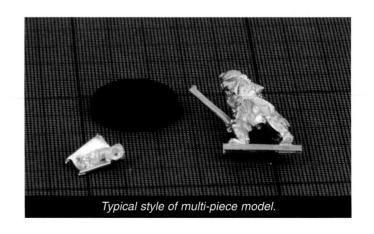

Typical style of multi-piece model.

The fit can usually be improved very quickly by filing the mating surfaces. Don't expect the join to be perfect, as this is practically impossible with metal castings produced from flexible rubber moulds. There will probably be slight gaps which can be filled once the pieces are joined.

If the model has a slottabase, make sure that the rail between the model's feet fits snugly into the slot. If the fit is very loose, use your pliers to slightly kink the rail so it grips the base adequately – this will help keep the model in position once you glue the base to it.

Some people will wash metal castings before assembly to remove any grease that can sometimes result from extensive handling. This should not really be necessary, but excess grease can affect the primer coat so it is worth doing if models have been handled a great deal.

Once you are happy with the fit, glue the pieces together using superglue. When joining metal pieces, use a small amount of glue and hold the surfaces together for a moment until it sets, then put the model down and allow the join to set more thoroughly.

A file is essential for adjusting to fit.

If the rail is loose, a kink will produce a tighter fit.

Assemble with superglue.

If you find that the pieces do not stick together straightaway, use plasticine or adhesive putty, such as Blu-tack, to hold them in place whilst the glue sets. Larger pieces may need additional support whilst drying, in which case try holding them with sticky tape or elastic bands.

Occasionally, a piece will just refuse to stick – possibly because too much glue has been applied to begin with. If a piece proves especially troublesome, it is sometimes worth using a blob of epoxy putty to stick it in place.

This is especially useful for fixing shields to Warhammer models because the blob won't be seen and shields need the extra support, as they are vulnerable to being knocked off.

Fixing a shield with Blu-tack.

Even if a shield is subsequently broken, it is easier to fix back if the warrior's hand preserves its putty attachment.

Superglue is also fine for fixing metal to plastic components, such as a model's base.

ASSEMBLING PLASTIC MODELS

Citadel plastic kits are moulded onto frames or 'sprues', so begin by checking over them to ensure that all the pieces are present and correct. Larger kits, such as the Space Marine Rhino and Land Raider, come with their own assembly instructions, but the trooper types consist of interchangeable components and can usually be assembled into a variety of poses. Whether you are assembling Warhammer regiments sets or Warhammer 40,000 squads, it's worth working out how you want the finished unit to look before gluing the models together. Remember that Warhammer models need to fit edge to edge against each other to make a unit, which will slightly limit the degree of animation.

It is often recommended that plastic sprues are washed in warm water containing a little mild detergent, such as washing up liquid – this is to remove any traces of oil that may have been applied to the steel mould during storage. This is a precaution rather than a necessity because any such oil will tend to end up on the first few models in the production run rather than the whole batch. However, as any trace of oil will resist the undercoat and make painting very difficult, it is worth taking the extra effort to remove it. Any grease that results from handling the pieces will also be removed, of course.

Remove pieces from the sprues as required and check for mould lines, detachment scars and fit. The moulds used to make plastic models are made of steel and precisely engineered, but even so the extremely high pressure of the plastic often results in some seepage between the mould halves. This results in a slight mould line that can be scraped off with a craft knife. As with metal models, pay extra attention where such lines are highly visible as they will show through the completed paint job.

A small detachment scar will be left where pieces have been removed from the sprue or where the pieces have associated 'ejectors' that allow them to be removed from the mould. Scrape these flat with a file. These scars are particularly noticeable on bases, so run a file along the edges of the plastic base to smooth out any irregularities.

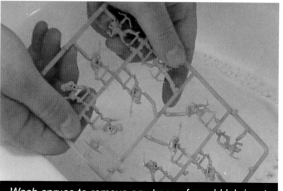
Wash sprues to remove any trace of mould lubricant.

Clippers are ideal for removing parts.

A file is essential for clean-up and fit adjustment.

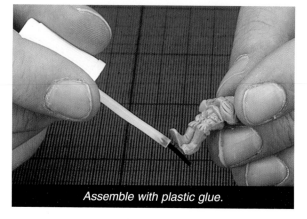
Assemble with plastic glue.

Arm positions can be adjusted by cutting away a section of the joining surface.

Plastic pieces should fit consistently well as produced, but you may prefer to slightly change the angle of an arm or head, or adjust the torso so that it inclines slightly forward or back – these are easy adjustments to make with plastic models. Use your craft knife to shave away part of the join or file away the mating surfaces to get the angle you want. Don't overdo things, though, as it's much easier to remove plastic than it is to put it back!

Once you are satisfied that pieces fit together, glue them in place using liquid polystyrene glue – or 'liquid poly' as it is known. Alternatively, you can use polystyrene cement, such as Citadel plastic glue, which is thicker and easier to apply, but liquid poly is better for small parts and generally superior once you have mastered its use. To apply liquid poly you will need a small brush – this is supplied with some brands of glue, otherwise use an old paint brush. Brush a little glue onto both surfaces to be joined and press them together – the glue will melt the surfaces together and produce a strong join. As polystyrene glue will melt any plastic it touches, it is important not to apply too much. If you do get glue onto the surface detail, it is best to allow it to dry and scrape or file away any excess rather than attempt to remove the glue whilst it is wet.

Cavalry models commonly feature plastic steeds with metal or plastic riders.

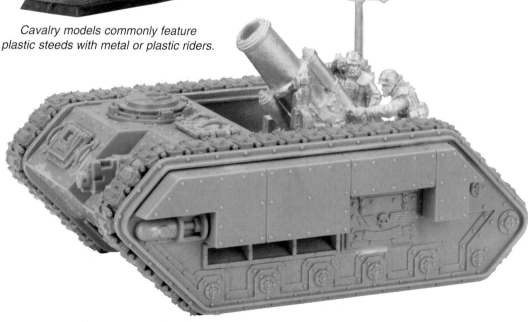

Vehicles often include metal as well as plastic components.

GAP FILLING

This book isn't chiefly concerned with modelling – a subject worthy of a volume in its own right – but if you are painting large multi-piece metal models then you will almost certainly need to do some minor gap filling. In fact, any slottabased model will usually have a gap where the model fits into its base, and it is worth filling these before applying a base texture or paint. In any case, filling gaps will improve the appearance of the finished models and help to make them stronger.

The two materials that we would recommend for gap filling are two-part epoxy putty and ordinary plasticine or similar soft modelling clay. Epoxy putty is by far the best and is absolutely necessary where a piece is going to be regularly handled. Plasticine is a good stop gap (ahem!) for filling tiny gaps in places that won't be directly handled such as under arms and for plugging holes in bases that are going to be textured over. You can, of course, mix up epoxy putty and use it for any and all filling,

but it's quicker and just as good to use plasticine in some situations. Plasticine does not harden, but once you have applied undercoat and painted the resultant skin, it is quite resilient. A tiny blob of superglue will also provide a hard skin to a plug of plasticine that will enable it to withstand moderate handling.

There are different brands of two-part epoxy on the market, but we would recommend only those sold specifically for modelling – those designed for plumbing and similar purposes tend to harden so quickly that they are difficult to use. The putty from the Citadel Modelling range comes in a two-coloured strip that contains both putty and hardener.

Large models always require more adjustment and gap filling where the pieces join.

Cut off a small piece and mix the two parts together until you have a consistent coloured putty. Because the components interact, you may find a layer of hard 'bits' where the two strip colours meet – if so, cut this narrow centre section of the strip out and throw it away before mixing.

To fill a long thin gap, make a thin sausage of putty and lay it over the gap. Push the putty into the gap using your knife or modelling tool if you have one. Trim any excess but aim to slightly overfill the gap – you can file the putty back later.

Let the putty cure – it will set faster if it is slightly warm. You will find that the putty will cure quite quickly if you place the bulb from your desk lamp about six inches over the model – do not place it too close or plastic components may melt!

To fill in broader gaps, such as those that occur under an arm that you might have repositioned, make a blob of about the right size and push into the gap with the end of a modelling tool or the tip of your knife. Try to blend the edges of the putty with the surrounding detail as much as possible. Cut away any excess and allow the putty to dry as before.

If you are filling in gaps over a highly textured surface, such as fur or hair, then you may wish to model back as much detail as possible to cover the join. This isn't especially hard in the case of a fur texture. If the texture is quite coarse, use the tip of your knife to draw out the putty into little ridges, trying to match the original as much as possible. If the texture is finer, such as hair, use the edge of the blade and draw long, fine strokes in the same direction as on the rest of the model. Mix up some putty and practise first if you are unsure of your abilities – from such humble beginnings comes many a Citadel Designer!

Gaps in slottabases can also be covered over with a piece of tape if you intend to apply a decorative texture to finish the model. This is very simple and quick, and the texture will completely cover over the tape.

Mix the putty and roll a small piece into a sausage or ball.

Push the putty into place with the tip of your modelling tool.

Modelling back hair is relatively easy and, once undercoated, is undetectable.

UNDERCOAT

If you are painting a regiment or squad then assemble the whole batch and allow all the glue or epoxy putty to dry thoroughly before going to the next stage.

To be safe, leave the models overnight to make sure all the glue is set – if you undercoat models before glue is completely set, the solvents in the undercoat can cause the pieces to become detached.

Some people like to apply a base texture before undercoating their models – this is described later on in the section about Bases. This is a matter of personal preference and depends to some extent on the kind of base finish that you favour.

If you texture your bases before undercoating, it is especially important to let the whole thing dry before applying an undercoat as otherwise the texture will lift.

An entire unit of Empire Halberdiers, assembled and under orders.

The same guys sprayed with a black undercoat.

The purpose of the undercoat is twofold: it acts as a primer, or 'key', and it provides a flat base colour to paint onto. You can undercoat with a brush using standard paint, but this will provide a weaker primer than a can of spray paint which is designed to 'key' to metal or plastic surfaces.

You will also find that the spray finish is far flatter and better to paint onto than a brushed undercoat which tends to give an uneven and slightly resistant surface.

Overall the benefits of using a spray undercoat far outweigh the cost, and if you are undercoating many models at once, the saving in time is worth it alone.

PREPARING TO SPRAY

Citadel Colour spray cans are designed for undercoating metal and plastic models – similar products for modellers are available from most hobby stores.

There is one important rule when using spray paints; namely, never ever use them in the house because the spray forms a fine mist that will coat everything nearby.

Only spray out of doors or in a well ventilated shed or similar outbuilding – open the door and a window to

A cardboard box makes a good spray booth... but put some newspaper down too!

get a good through draft if possible. This is not only best for you, it is best for the work too because the undercoat will dry almost instantly on the models and form a slightly textured surface that holds paint well. However, very hot or cold conditions can sometimes affect the paint, so take extra care to read the instructions if you are using spray cans in these circumstances.

The ideal place to spray is a workshop, garage or shed with a work surface or similar table. Cover the whole surface with newspaper. Make sure there is nothing nearby that might get damaged – eg, bicycle, lawnmower, car, washing machine. If this is unavoidable, cover up with a dust sheet. Most importantly of all, don't use an inflammable spray anywhere near a naked flame, for example, the pilot light of a boiler. I know this all sounds very obvious but it always sounds obvious after the event, doesn't it!

If you place models directly onto the work surface and spray them, you'll find the paint forms a fine mist that goes everywhere – this is called 'overspray'. To prevent this you will need to make some kind of booth into

which you can place the models and which will serve to contain most of the overspray. This need be no more elaborate than a cardboard box turned onto its side, or you can use pieces of card to make a shield around the spraying area.

If you are obliged to spray on the floor, the same precautions apply – lay down plenty of paper to catch the overspray. If you spray outside, choose a calm day and a spot where any overspray won't cause damage. Bear in mind that it is very difficult to shift paint from concrete, patios and paving, whilst grass does grow back eventually – 'nuff said!

Texture the base and undercoat the whole model in one go.

UNDERCOAT COLOUR

The colour required depends on the subject and your preferred technique, but most people will use a white or black undercoat. Although you can buy other spray colours, these are best applied as base colours over an undercoat rather than used as an undercoat themselves.

White provides a good undercoat for general use as it makes an excellent base for applying other colours. Most beginners start with a white undercoat as it gives the ideal 'blank canvas', and you don't need to master any special techniques to get a good result. At the other end of the scale, the most experienced painters tend to favour white as an undercoat because it's ideal for applying the various blending techniques and gives the cleanest colours. A white undercoat always gives the brightest finished colour and is therefore necessary if you wish to paint bright yellows or reds.

A white undercoat works well for models that are predominantly pale or brightly coloured.

Vehicles with large flat areas are often easier to paint using a white undercoat.

*A black undercoat also works
as the basic shading layer.*

Black is often used by people who want good results relatively quickly and, as such, is ideally suited to painting a large number of models at one go. The chief advantage of a black undercoat is that the deepest recesses can be left black to provide the darkest level of shading – this gives a very pleasing look without a great deal of effort. However, some colours don't paint well over black, and all colours will tend to look less bright, which means it is sometimes necessary to repaint selected areas white and then apply your chosen colour. We'll come back to this in detail in the Techniques section. For now, think of black undercoats as best for mass painting and for painting models that are going to end up very dark or black, such as Dark Angels or Black Templar Space Marines.

However, much depends on your personal technique and many people find black or white undercoats give them perfectly satisfactory results in these cases.

SPRAYING

Place the models to be sprayed on a piece of card and put them into your spraying booth or onto the newspaper. Apply your chosen colour lightly over the models – there is no need to soak the models with paint; just aim for a light overall cover. If you use too much paint, it will run and can form visible pools once dry. When you have sprayed from one direction, turn the piece of card round and spray from the opposite side – this is why it's a good idea to place the models onto card otherwise you need to handle the models themselves. Sometimes you will need to spray from several different angles to catch all the recessed surfaces.

Leave the models to dry and then check to make sure you have caught the areas under arms, legs and beneath weapons. Usually you will have missed some bits, so lay the models down and spray again from the underside. This is especially important with models that have outstretched wings, shields or overhanging backpacks as it is impossible to cover all the undersides from above. Aim to get an even light coat over the entire model, but don't worry if there is a little metal or plastic showing in the undercuts as these can be touched in later.

Once the undercoat is thoroughly dry, the models are ready to start painting. If you are painting a group of models, perhaps a Warhammer regiment for example, or even a whole army, then it is worth preparing and undercoating everything at once. You will find that you need to use almost as much spray paint to undercoat a single model as a group, so most people tend to save up a batch and do all the undercoating in a single session. Not only is this the most economical and efficient method but it is a great feeling having a whole regiment sat ready on your painting table ready to go!

Spray paints can be affected by extreme temperatures resulting in a powdery finish or a pale bloom in the case of black – always read the guide instructions on the can. If in doubt, test the spray on a piece of scrap first.

TECHNIQUES

In this section we'll be taking a look at the various techniques employed to paint miniatures. In order to cover a wide range of techniques, the information has been organised alphabetically by subject and cross-referenced where it was felt helpful to do so. It is not a step-by-step guide but a guide to techniques of all kinds. A series of comprehensive step-by-step examples are given towards the end of the book and serve as a demonstration of the various techniques.

Some techniques are easier to master than others, but good results are not necessarily dependent upon the time taken or even the painter's technical skill. Some approaches are far more time consuming than others and are therefore only appropriate for painting relatively small numbers of models – for example, blending can be very laborious. On the other hand, the most dramatic effects can often be executed extremely quickly. Whatever techniques you use, the trick is to apply them with style!

AIM

It's not a bad thing to occasionally remind ourselves why we are painting a particular model or series of models. Is it a model for display, a competition entry, or a new recruit into the ranks of our armies? The destiny you have in mind for the completed model will naturally dictate the process. A model prepared for competition might take several months to complete, but an army that progressed at that rate would never reach the battlefield. If your aim is to produce armies then the first thing to do is not set yourself an impossibly high standard. If you want an army to game with then a finished army beats an unfinished army every time. Furthermore, the more armies you paint, the faster and better you get because you are learning all the time, so don't get hung up trying to make everything perfect – it's a common source of frustration and not just amongst beginners either!

BASIC BRUSHWORK

Choose a brush of a size that you feel comfortable using. A good brush will come to a point whatever its size. A small brush is handier when it comes to hard to reach places, and is better for fine control simply because the shorter bristles are more rigid. A larger brush holds more paint and will be better for painting large areas in one go.

Wet and point the brush before using it – you can use water or plain old spit – removing any excess by drawing the brush over a piece of tissue, a cloth, the palette or your fingers. If you gently twist the brush as you do this, it will naturally come to a point. You will occasionally need to repoint the brush as you paint. Some people routinely lick the brushes into points – whilst walking around with paint all over your lips may hinder your social life, it is reassuring to know that Citadel Colour paints are non-toxic.

Beginners sometimes worry too much about being neat – some experienced painters produce models that look very messy right up until the final brushstroke and then miraculously turn into masterpieces!

It is a sign of good brush control that you can place the paint where you want it – but don't worry too much if the paint strays onto an adjacent unpainted area as this will get covered over later. This is something that comes quickly with practise.

PAINTING REGIMENTS
Dave Andrews

"I wanted to create an effective looking force but one that was quick to finish. To do this I painted every model in the army at the same time, applying a basecoat to each figure before moving on to the next stage. The hieroglyphs on the scrolls and shields were photocopies from a source book which were then reduced – a simple but very effective technique."

BLACK UNDERCOATS

Working With Black

If you are going to paint a whole army then it is well worth learning how to paint over a black undercoat. It's probably fair to say that this is the standard mass painting technique, though many excellent miniature artists use the same method to paint individual models for display. It is a fast and fairly undemanding system that is relatively easy to learn and produces very good results.

If you're not sure whether a colour is going to make a good dark or light shade, experiment using a piece of white card first. The Citadel Colour range includes progressive shades of colours.

If you have a dark and a light colour an easy way of creating a harmonious mid-tone is simply to mix them together – this mix will blend visually with both. For the lightest highlights simply add white (see 'Highlights').

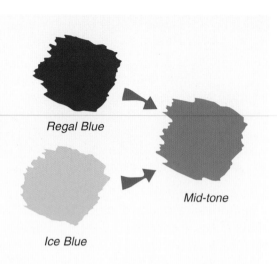

Regal Blue

Mid-tone

Ice Blue

The whole model is worked up from a black undercoat base by applying successive layers, starting with dark shade colours and progressing to light highlight colours.

● *Chaos Black*

● *Midnight Blue*

● *Enchanted Blue*

Take the example of a cloak that is to be blue. Begin by painting a deep blue over the area but leave black in the deepest recesses to form the darkest level of shade. Then apply a lighter blue colour over the high relief on the cloak but leave a line of the dark blue between the black and the lighter blue.

This is basic 'layering' using two colours over black, but the technique can be extended with multiple layers to produce a more subtle effect (see 'Layering' for more about this).

This two-tone layering technique is probably the most time effective way of producing armies that look good on the tabletop.

The secret of working from black is to use the right colours and to leave enough of each layer visible to produce the required effect. Experimentation is the best way to learn. Remember that you may prefer a lighter or darker look than someone else, and you may find that some armies look better overall dark than overall light – a good painter will vary the look to suit the subject.

It is very hard to paint a bright red over black without under-painting the whole area first in a solid white or mix of red and white.

However, in most cases a more muted red is to be preferred, and this can be worked up in the usual way from a deep red colour to a brighter red.

Use a deep red colour, such as Red Gore, covering the greater portion of the area and leaving black in only the deepest recesses and along the delineating edges.

● *Chaos Black*   ● *Red Gore*   ● *Blood Red*

● *Chaos Black*   ◐ *Snakebite Leather & Golden Yellow*   ○ *Golden Yellow*

Next layer a warm red, such as Blood Red (or Blood Red + Blazing Orange or Blood Red + any Yellow) leaving a narrow band of the darker red. This layer will look darker than the paint colour but the final effect is a pleasing muted red.

A similar technique can be applied to painting yellow for a slightly warm/ochre colour which looks very good on cloth. In this case, begin with a layer of Snakebite Leather and Golden Yellow and apply a second layer of Golden Yellow or Sunburst Yellow.

● *Chaos Black*   ● *Dark Flesh*   ◐ *Dwarf Flesh*   ○ *Elf Flesh*

To work up a face from black, first apply Dark Flesh leaving the eyes and any extremely deep creases black. Next paint a layer of Dwarf Flesh over the face leaving the Dark Flesh in the creases, such as around the eyes, mouth, nose, etc, – this will vary depending on the face.

Finally, because the face is the focal point of a model, paint the highest points on the face Elf Flesh – generally the bridge and wings of the nose, the chin, the top of the cheekbones and the jawline.

BLENDING

The basis of blending is to apply a highlight to a dry base colour and then, whilst the paint is still wet, to fade out the hard edge by drawing out the paint thinly.

Blending is not, as the name might suggest, mixing two wet colours together on the model. The idea is to draw out the edge of the highlight colour so that it blends into the colour beneath. This process of drawing out the paint is also known as 'feathering'.

Most painters will blend colours together in the way described without necessarily being conscious of the fact – it is a natural result of the translucent quality of the paint itself.

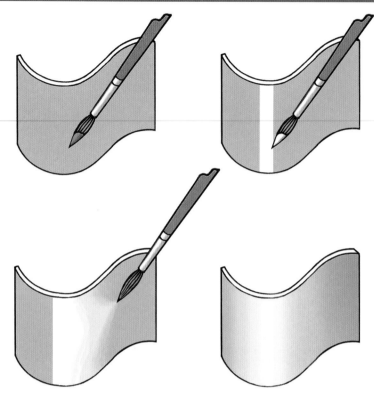

To blend, first paint a line or area over the base coat, then draw out the paint. Draw the paint out more thinly as you go so that it blends into the colour beneath.

Many painters who use a layering technique tend to blend the colours together as they go. A few, however, prefer the other extreme, making the individual layers very distinct to produce a deliberately striated appearance.

Blending allows the painter to control the effect very exactly and is therefore a very commonly seen technique on winners of painting competitions, such as Golden Demon. It is, however, a long and painstaking process, and it takes many hours of patient work to fully blend a model in this way.

It is a technique that lends itself well to photography – giving a very favourable impression of the method in books such as this!

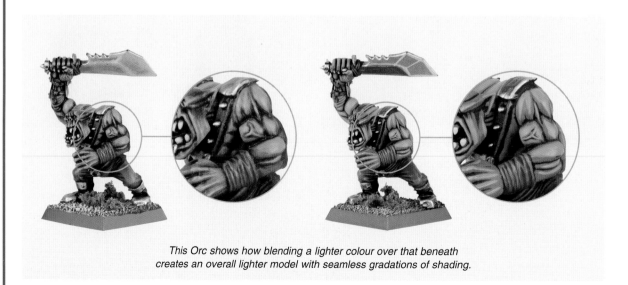

This Orc shows how blending a lighter colour over that beneath creates an overall lighter model with seamless gradations of shading.

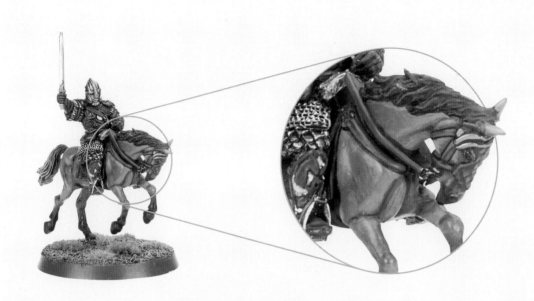

Careful blending brings this model to life.

However, it must be accepted that the overall appearance of an army painted in this way is comparable to an army painted using more rapid wash or layering techniques. The appearance of an army depends much more on the artist's sense of style and colour than upon time consuming technique. The ability to blend does not in itself make an expert painter!

The most careful application of the blending technique requires two brushes – one to apply paint and one to feather the paint. Both brushes must be small (Citadel Detail or Fine Detail) and well pointed.

Mix a suitable highlight colour and paint it onto the area you want to highlight – bear in mind that the blending process will spread the paint slightly. The paint mix must be fairly thin to enable it to be drawn out easily, so add a little water.

Judging exactly how thin the paint needs to be is quite difficult and only comes with practise –

inexperienced painters will commonly use paint that is too thick. Wet the second brush with clean water and bring to a point (it is most effective to dampen and point this brush with your lips as you work). Use the brush to carefully draw out the paint and feather the edge to blend the colour into that beneath.

Using two brushes to blend.

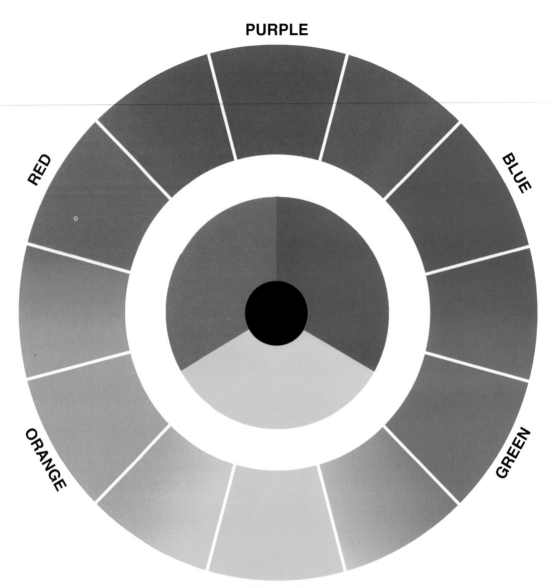

COLOUR THEORY

For our purposes there is little to be gained by studying colour theory in depth – and should you wish to do so there are plenty of books devoted to the concept. However, it is worth going through some of the basics to explain the idea behind colour theory and some of the terminology.

As everyone knows there are three primary colours – red, yellow and blue – which theoretically make black when combined together in equal proportion. By mixing the primaries in pairs we produce three further colours – orange, purple and green. By varying the proportion of the mix, we have gradations of reddish or yellowish oranges, bluish or reddish purples, and yellowish or bluish greens. The colour wheel shown above demonstrates this.

In terms of the colour wheel, colours that are opposite are described as **complementary,** so red complements green, blue complements orange, and yellow complements purple. By mixing a small amount of the complementary colour into a chosen colour you will darken it (as you are combining all three primaries).

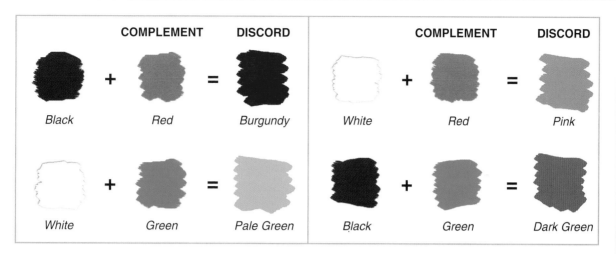

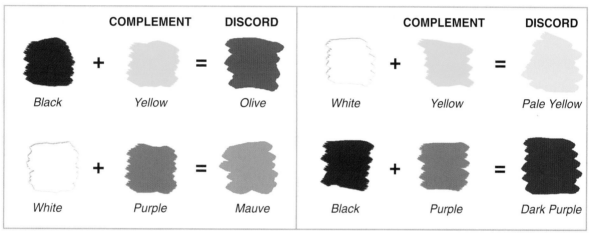

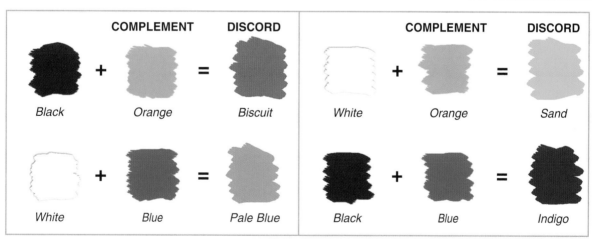

Colours that are adjacent on the colour wheel are described as **harmonies** – the harmonies of red are orange and purple, for example. These colours blend together naturally because they lie next to each other on the colour wheel. By taking sets of complements and adding black to one and white to the other you obtain a series of **discords**. Discords are extreme contrasts –

they can work very well where you want a model's costume to have a contrasting trim colour, for example. Colour theory is based on theoretical pure colours, so you will not always obtain a clean colour by mixing the equivalent paints. Most red paints already contain some yellow, whilst greens and blues may contain white. Often you'll need to use a specific paint to get clean colours.

DRYBRUSHING

A drybrush technique is a fast and attractive way of adding highlights to areas of raised detail. It can also be used to apply a fine texture to large flat areas such as armour plating to create a realistic effect. A light drybrush over an entire model can give it an overall dusting that draws the colours together and gives a natural appearance.

Drybrushing is often confused with the very similar technique which we have deliberately described separately as 'overbrushing'. The difference is simply that drybrushing uses a drybrush whilst overbrushing does not – but the two techniques tend to merge into each other and most painters combine the techniques as they work.

Drybrushing is most easily demonstrated by painting a hair or fur texture. Begin with a suitable base colour that has been shaded with a wash if required – the drybrushing is added at the final stage to provide highlights.

Take the brush (preferably an old brush) and mix up a light shade of the base colour. The paint needs to be fairly dense. If the paint is a little thin, let it dry slightly on the palette. Work the colour into the brush and then wipe any excess back onto the palette.

Now – most importantly – run the brush over a tissue or newspaper, or some similarly absorbent surface, until the strokes leave almost no mark even when applied with pressure. Depending on the effect you want, you can make the brush more or less dry.

Begin by stroking the brush gently over the surface that you wish to highlight. Ideally the brush should leave no discernible strokes, but only deposits a fine, even dusting of colour over the high points on the model. The drier the brush, the more the effect will appear as a dusting of even colour. Build up the highlights gradually and notice how repeated dusting gives naturally gradated highlights. The longer you work at the result, the more intense the effect.

Several progressively lighter layers of drybrushing can be applied to increase contrast – the final layer can be white.

Drybrushing wears brushes out extremely quickly which is why the Citadel range includes special hard-wearing brushes for just this purpose. Any old brush can be pressed into service – cut down the bristles slightly if they are still fairly long. The dryer and more finely you drybrush, the more quickly your brushes will wear down or become too badly splayed to use.

Load the brush with paint.

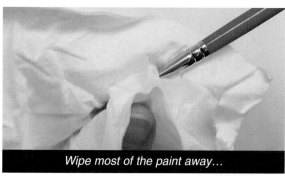

Wipe most of the paint away…

… until the brush leaves almost no mark.

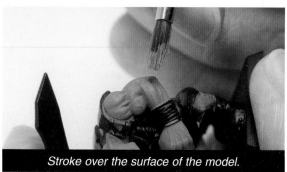

Stroke over the surface of the model.

If you drybrush over a fairly bright colour, the result can sometimes look very chalky. If you want to restore colour while retaining the highlighting, apply a wash of ink as described in the section on 'Glazes'.

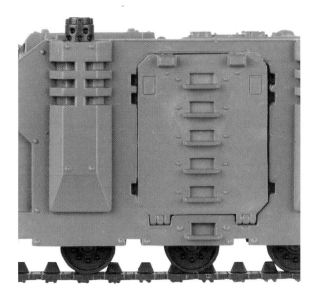

Rhino – the armour plates have been drybrushed with an extremely dry brush to produce a realistic lightly textured finish.

If you are drybrushing a large flatish area, such as part of a vehicle, the effect will work best if you use a very dry brush so that it is necessary to scrub quite hard to deposit any colour on the surface. This doesn't do the brushes very much good – brushes used in this way will quickly wear out.

Drybrushing works very well on highly textured surfaces such as the fur on the boar pictured below.

The process can be a little messy, so it's worth painting a subject like this with the rider off.

Boar – heavy fur textures can be easily and quickly drybrushed.

Cadian Imperial Guard regiment – before and after drybrushing.

If you like the realistic, slightly faded or 'light drenched' look that drybrushing confers, the technique can be gently applied to the entire model as a final stage.

This will give the model an overall dusting that helps to draw the colours together and tone down any harsh shades. This can be very pleasing in an army, and many people find the look far more convincing than bright shiny colours.

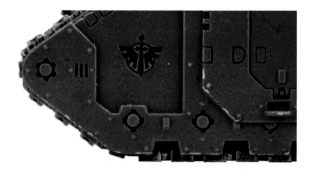

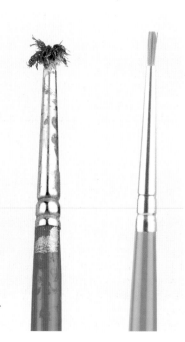

Drybrushing wears out brushes, so it is best to use old brushes that have already lost their points.

Cut down the tip to a flat end – this works better than a conventional pointed tip.

Warhammer 40,000 fighting vehicles don't have to look as if they've just been driven out of the Adeptus showroom – drybrushing can be applied to represent fading and weathering, or more heavily with grubby browns to indicate dust, dirt and mud.

EYES

There's more than one way to represent eyes depending on what kind of result you are looking for. In reality, you don't notice people's eyes if they are ten yards away and certainly not at a hundred yards or more. If this is the case, there's no reason why a model's eyes have to be noticeable at several feet away – the typical distance at which a model is likely to be viewed.

For most purposes, simply shading in the eye area will be quite sufficient. However, there will undoubtedly be occasions when you want to add eye detail to a model, if only because you can! Large models with correspondingly large eyes also benefit from

having the eyes detailed in some fashion.

When painting eyes, begin by applying a deep shade to the whole eye socket area – the actual tone depends on the effect you wish to achieve. Darker and redder tones make the eyes look more sunken and work well for 'evil' faces. Then, carefully paint the eye black using a small well-pointed brush. If you make a mistake, don't worry – it's easy to correct the shape of the eye at the final stage.

For 'evil' creatures you can create a very effective look by painting a single small white dot into the centre of the eye rather than into the corners – this gives the model a wild, manic appearance.

Apply a touch of white into the left and right corners of each eye. Try to match the left and right eyes as closely as possible, but don't worry too much as you can add in a little black to reduce the amount of white showing if necessary.

Finally, if you feel it is necessary to tidy the face up, paint a flesh tone back onto the eyelids and under the eyes, leaving enough shading to give definition.

Broadly speaking it isn't necessary to paint the eyes on a human sized model – you won't see a real person's eyes at typical tabletop distances so it is perfectly realistic to simply shade the whole eye area. If you must paint eyes then try not to make them too large or staring – the less visible the white, the more convincing the effect. If you want the model to look wild eyed and crazed then paint more white! Horses only show white in their eyes when they are wild or panicked.

For larger models, or a more detailed effect in any scale, you can paint the eyes using the following method – but be warned this takes a little longer and won't be noticeably different unless you are going to be looking at your models very closely indeed.

Begin by shading the eye sockets and area around the eyes as before. If your shading isn't particularly dark, mix a very dark shade colour and paint in the eye to define the outline of each eye.

Once any shading is dry, carefully paint in the shape of each eye in white. Try to get the eyes the same shape and size.

Dot in the pupils using black. Unless you want the model to appear particularly fixated, try to place the pupils slightly over the mid-point of each eye so that there is no white showing above the pupils. Try and match the eyes as closely as possible. A fibre-tipped pen is an alternative way of doing this.

Finally, if you have painted the whites slightly large or unevenly, mix up your shade colour and repaint around the eyes to reduce or match them. Once this is dry, repaint flesh colour around the eyelids and sockets, allowing the shade colour to remain in the creases to give definition.

If a model is especially large then painting the eyes is obviously more important. In this case, it may be beneficial to add a separate iris colour and to apply highlights onto the iris or pupil itself. However fiddly this might seem, there is no secret to the technique other than care and patience.

FLAT COLOUR

When you apply a single solid colour onto your undercoat, the result is a flat colour – an even coverage with no shading, highlighting or other effects. In some cases two light coats of paint may be needed to achieve a uniform flat colour – this gives better results than a single very heavy coat which will obscure detail.

Many beginners will instinctively paint a whole model in flat colours – all the flesh is painted in a single flesh colour, all the coat in a uniform coat colour, a belt in a uniform brown, and so on.

This isn't a bad way to learn basic brushwork and the result can be quite acceptable. However, adding a few simple tricks such as a 'wash' will transform a model's appearance dramatically.

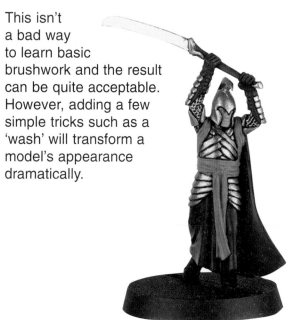

Elven warrior from The Lord of The Rings range.

GLAZES

A glaze is used to intensify colour, or restore strong colour, by applying a layer of strongly coloured ink. Unlike paint, ink is transparent and so allows the underlying colour, and any shading or highlighting, to show through. A glaze is also a good way of emphasising gemstones, wax seals, or similar decorative parts of the model which you want to stand out.

A glaze is also a suitable method for restoring the overall appearance to an area that has been highlighted too much, for example, by over-enthusiastic drybrushing. If you want to subtly reinforce a colour, mix ink with water and then glaze over the underlying paint with as many separate coats as needed – this enables you to gauge the effect as you go. If using very thin glazes to reinforce underlying colour, it can help to mix a little soap (washing up liquid) into the ink as this will break the surface tension and helps the ink cover evenly without forming puddles or patches.

Any ink glaze will leave a gloss surface, ideal for shiny gems but not necessarily desirable for everything. If an overall matt varnish is going to be applied to the finished model this will, of course, remove the gloss effect. If you want to preserve the gloss

The before and after effect of a Yellow Ink glaze on an Orc.

effect, either apply the glaze over the top of the matt layer or selectively apply a final gloss varnish on top of the matt layer.

To some extent, wash and glaze effects can amount to the same thing, as both use ink to recolour the paint beneath. The difference is that a glaze should ideally be an even, thin coat whilst a wash is applied liberally and allowed to run into recesses on the model. To a degree it's impossible to do one without doing the other as all but the thinnest glaze will gather into low points, whilst a wash will glaze any high points.

Glazes using paint mixes are less effective but can also work – see the section on 'Washes' for hints about mixing up paints into suitable washes.

  ● *Fiery Orange*   ○ *Drybrush Skull White*   ◐ *Glaze Yellow Ink*

Glazing is one of the best methods of creating a strong yellow colour that has some depth to it. Begin with an orange and then drybrush using white to create highlights before finally glazing the whole area with Yellow Ink. This creates a strong yellow with shading and highlighting. Additional glazes of ink can be applied to create a more intense colour if necessary.

GUIDE COAT

If a model is undercoated white it can be quite difficult to see all the detail because the surface is so bright and uniform. To get round this, some painters will paint on a guide coat – a thin wash of a dark colour applied over the whole model to show up the details. The aim is simply to create a visual guide for further paintwork. Because the paint will gather into folds and creases, it usefully indicates shadowed areas as well as distinguishing details. Using thinned down ink, or adding a little varnish to the wash mix, will enhance this effect as discussed under Washes.

A guide coat readily exposes the detail of this Eldar.

HIGHLIGHTS

Extreme Highlights

Extreme highlights will usually occur only on hard edged regular surfaces such as the edges of swords and guns, large armour plates (such as shoulder pads) and on vehicles. Extreme highlights are usually indicated as a very thin line of white or silver (or a very pale highlight colour) on the very edge of the piece. The idea is to produce a hard line that emphasises the contrast between illuminated and shadowed surfaces.

When applying extreme highlights, it is important to keep in mind the theoretical position of your light source. There are two

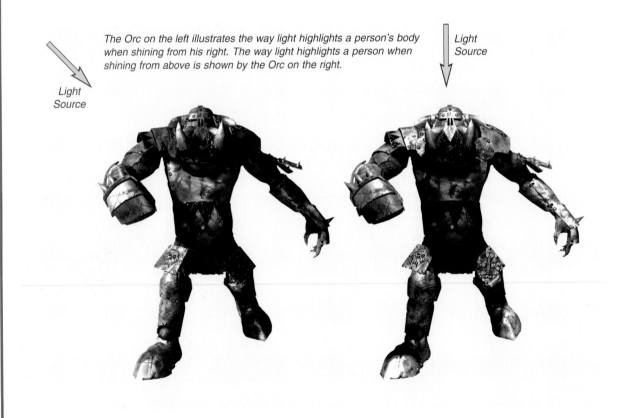

The Orc on the left illustrates the way light highlights a person's body when shining from his right. The way light highlights a person when shining from above is shown by the Orc on the right.

Light Source

Light Source

basic systems – one is to assume that the light is coming from a single fixed point, the other is to assume that the light is coming from a halo positioned above the model. The first will look more natural but means that the model will look 'right' from only one viewing position. The second is slightly false but works well where models are primarily viewed from different angles and from above.

Apply the extreme highlights using as fine a line as possible, catching only the illuminated edge of the subject. Some painters will blend this line onto the lit edge – this is best done in two stages. Apply the hard white line first and allow to dry. Then, thin the paint, reapply the line and blend towards the base colour. This creates a contrast between the extreme highlight and the blending which mimics the way light falls on hard edged surfaces.

Hard edges show extreme highlights on this gun mount.

Space Marine power armour is a natural subject for an extreme highlight and worth looking at in detail.

Dark Angels Space Marine

Blood Angels Space Marine

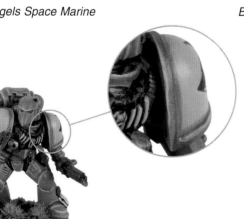

Space Wolves Space Marine

Black Templars Space Marine

LAYERING

Multi-layering Techniques

Layering is a technique of representing shade and highlights by painting successive gradations of a colour from dark to light (we have already seen how this works in the section on 'Black Undercoats'). Two-tone layering over a black undercoat provides shading and highlighting and looks effective from any reasonable distance. In principle the technique can be used with any undercoat and can be refined to the point where individual layers become indistinguishable even from very close up. A multi-tone layering technique taken to its ultimate form gives results that are comparable

to a fully blended technique, but there are many situations where an extra layer will help to give definition to a model.

The most difficult thing about all layering techniques is colour choice – it is important to choose shades that work well together over your undercoat colour. Here are a few basic samples of common colour combinations. In addition, see the Mixing chart on page 45.

A sophisticated multi-layer technique relies on mixing the colours together in different proportions to produce intermediate shades. The colour samples shown alongside illustrate this quite well. So, to take an example, to multi-layer Ultramarines Blue (UB) to Enchanted Blue (EB) in three

Examples of models painted using layering techniques – Spearman, Chaos Marauder, Swordsman, Archer.

MULTI-LAYERING

Ultramarines Blue to Enchanted Blue
1st layer: UB
2nd layer: 2UB/1EB
3rd layer: 1UB/1EB
4th layer: 1UB/2EB
5th layer: EB

Blood Red to Blazing Orange
1st layer: BR
2nd layer: 2BR/1BO
3rd layer: 1BR/1BO
4th layer: 1BR/2BO
5th layer: BO

Fiery Orange to Golden Yellow
1st layer: FO
2nd layer: 2FO/1GY
3rd layer: 1FO/1GY
4th layer: 1FO/2GY
5th layer: GY

Snot Green to Goblin Green
1st layer: SG
2nd layer: 2SG/1GG
3rd layer: 1SG/1GG
4th layer: 1SG/2GG
5th layer: GG

intermediate stages the 1st layer is UB, the 2nd is a mix of 2UB/1EB, the 3rd is 1UB/1EB, the 4th is 1UB/2EB and the 5th is EB. In our samples the effect is a succession of stripes, but if the stripes are sufficiently narrow then the eye ceases to distinguish the individual shades even from close up.

Although layering can be used to produce a seamless gradation between one colour and another, it can also be used to produce a dramatic contrast. Many people find this 'stripy' style very pleasing when well executed. That means choosing colours that work together despite the differences in shade. Dramatic layering rarely uses more than three layers and some examples of

useful colour combinations are shown below. If you look at the Citadel Colour range you can work out dramatic contrasts by taking a root colour and picking out the midtone and one of the lightest colours in the series.

Many people find it quite difficult to get good results with very bright colours using this technique because the colours are hard to tone together. A way of getting colours to tone together better is to mix a little of the adjoining colour/s into the paint for each layer. Another way to make all the colours slightly pastel is by adding a little of the same very pale neutral colour such as Rotting Flesh, Fortress Grey, Bleached Bone or Skull White – this will draw all the colours together.

DRAMATIC LAYERING

Scorched Brown
Snakebite Leather
Bronzed Flesh

Scab Red
Blood Red
Fiery Orange

Regal Blue
Ice Blue
Skull White

Dark Angels Green
Scorpion Green
Scorpion Green
& Skull White

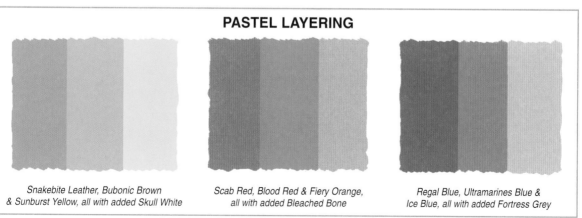

PASTEL LAYERING

Snakebite Leather, Bubonic Brown
& Sunburst Yellow, all with added Skull White

Scab Red, Blood Red & Fiery Orange,
all with added Bleached Bone

Regal Blue, Ultramarines Blue &
Ice Blue, all with added Fortress Grey

LINING-IN

Lining-in is a method of adding a hard dividing line between two parts of a model – usually where a hard shadow would naturally appear, for example between a cuff and hand or at the edges of a belt or strap.

Lining-in helps to emphasise the contrast between metal, wood, and flesh areas.

Extensive lining-in can be used over flat colours to produce a very clean, stark look. This is an effect seen rarely these days and which might reasonably be described as old-fashioned – having been superceded by more sophisticated shading techniques.

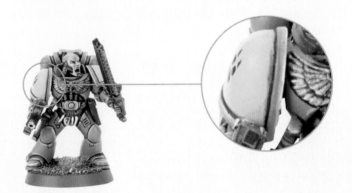

Lining-in makes a clear delineation around the shoulder pad rim.

Occasional lining-in is useful to add a stark contrast in selective areas – especially where shadow has perhaps been painted over accidentally.

In this usage, it is a way of applying finishing touches to a model that is essentially complete but needs some extra definition.

The technique is easy enough. Take some black paint and add water to produce a fluid but reasonably dense mix – somewhere between a 'wash' and normal paint consistency.

Some people use ink for lining-in, or a mixture of ink and paint, as this provides a denser line than diluted paint alone. Some people also add a little brown to the mix, but this depends on the desired effect and is purely a matter of taste.

Use a small brush with a good point and simply paint a thin black line where cuffs meet hands, around belts, collars, boot tops, and so on, adding a hard line to divide one area from the next. A fibre-tip pen can also be used.

Did you know... in many cases it takes longer for a Games Workshop 'Eavy Metal painter to paint a model than it took for the sculptor to make it in the first place! No wonder so few of them have armies – but when models have to be painted for box cover photographs they really do have to be the very best.

Not everyone can afford to be so lavish with their time of course. Even so, a decent sized army is going to take a while to complete so it's best to start off with the basic troop types. These will usually be the easiest to finish and, as you need them anyway, it makes sense to get the core of your army ready so you can start to use it as soon as possible.

METALLIC PAINTS

Metallic paints are unlike other paints in that they actually contain very finely ground flakes of metal – generally aluminium. Once dry, these bind with the transparent acrylic medium and give a good metallic appearance.

The metal flakes don't dissolve in the acrylic medium – if you dip your brush into some metallic paint and then in a pot of clean water you'll see how the metal flakes disperse over the water surface. If you use the same water pot for metallics and other paints then there is a tendency for the metal flakes to stay in the brush and get into other colours, and for this reason many painters use a separate water pot for metallic paint. Another solution is simply to change the water when it gets discoloured and make sure you rinse brushes well after using metallic paint.

All acrylic metallic paint is basically silver flake plus medium plus a pigment. Citadel Mithril Silver is the basic metal colour – all the other metallics are coloured by the addition of a pigment. For this reason, when you add water to a metallic paint it tends to become increasingly silver-ish as the pigment is diluted. Similarly, you can create almost any metallic colour by adding paint or ink to silver. Chainmail and Boltgun Metal are simply pre-mixes of silver and black. Because of the tendency of the pigment and metal flake to separate, it is a good idea to give the pots a good shake before opening.

Grey Knight Terminator

Empire Knight Templar

Any metallic colour can be lightened for highlights by adding silver, and silver can be used for the highest highlights. Metallic colours can be shaded by adding an appropriate dark paint to the mix or by washing with a dark ink. Metallic colours can be strengthened or tinted by glazing with a suitable ink colour.

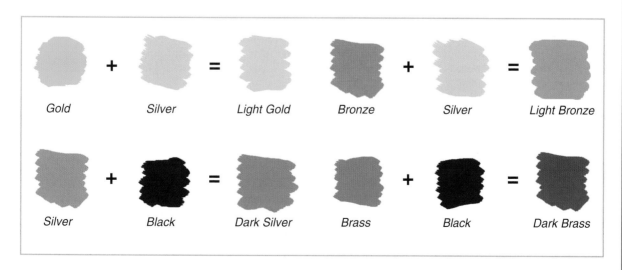

| Gold | + | Silver | = | Light Gold | Bronze | + | Silver | = | Light Bronze |
| Silver | + | Black | = | Dark Silver | Brass | + | Black | = | Dark Brass |

MIXING PAINT

Many otherwise competent painters seem to have trouble mixing paints – probably because they lack the confidence to do so. Be bold – if you never try you will never learn and you will be stuck with a limited selection of pre-mixed colours. Paints are made to be mixed – it is their destiny and it is our role to help them fulfil it.

By mixing paints together you can create colours that naturally tone together or 'harmonise'. This is fundamental to successful layering and blending as discussed elsewhere.

Most people will mix paint at some time if only to lighten or darken the basic colours, in which case beginners will often add white or black. Although there are some colours where this works, in most cases the result is simply to make a colour look chalky or pastel in the case of white, or dull and dirty in the case of black. The secret to painting highlights is to use a colour that is brighter, rather than merely lighter, whilst in the case of shades the ideal colour is deeper and more intense, rather than merely darker.

Here are some basic mixing principles for common colours. If you look at the Mixing Chart opposite you will notice that the various colour series are organised from the darkest to lightest shades, with suitable mix colours indicated at the end of each series.

Black – Adding white to black creates a very unnatural grey. If you also add a little of any mid-brown, or even a neutral mix of green and red, the grey will appear warmer and less mechanical.

White – Adding any colour to white will create a shade, but most people would add black or grey which can look unnatural. A more neutral shade can be achieved by adding a mix of grey and brown, or even a neutral mix of red and green. Shades of white and brown tend to work better with neutral or yellowish browns rather than red-based browns which will look pink.

Blue – Blues need to be shaded with deeper blues rather than black, as adding black will make the blue look very grubby. Blues can be lightened by adding white, but intense blues become chalky if you do this. It is better to lighten strong blues with a light blue first.

Red – To darken a strong red, add a strong green. Add a tiny amount and judge the effect – a little green darkens a lot of red. You can also darken a red using a dark red brown (Dark Flesh) in which case the result is a rather brownish red. Red can also be darkened effectively using black to produce a distinct 'burgundy' colour. Lightening a red is more difficult – add yellow and you get orange, add white and you get pink! Even worse if you add both you get a rather fleshy salmon colour. For most purposes, strong reds are best lightened with orange or yellow, but be wary of overdoing it.

Green – Greens are rather like blues in that they need to be shaded with deeper versions of the same colour rather than black. You can also deepen a strong green by adding a little red. Greens are very easy and pleasing colours to mix into lighter shades – you can add yellow, white, or even grey to make different shades without compromising the underlying colour.

Yellow – Yellows need to be shaded by mixing in yellow-based browns, orange or reds – basically warm colours. Adding black to yellow produces olive green – this is something to be careful of when mixing black into any yellowish browns too. To lighten yellow simply add white.

Browns – Can be quite hard to mix into toning light and dark colours. Yellow browns can be lightened by adding white, and darkened with deeper red browns. Red browns can be lightened by adding a light yellow brown or darkened by dark red browns or, if very dark, black. Adding white to red browns makes them unpleasantly pinkish. Neutral browns can also be lightened with grey, but beware if they are yellow-based as this may make them appear green (this is especially apparent when painting horses!).

When mixing paint try to mix up enough to cover the whole batch of models you are working on. A slightly dished palette such as a plate or saucer is better for this than a tile as it holds a decent depth of paint and so won't dry out too fast. If you do run out, mix a second batch beside the original (rather than on top of it) and do so before you actually run out. This enables you to match the colour whilst the original paint is wet. This is important because wet and dry colours always vary slightly. Finally, mix the old and new batches together to get as good a match as you can, but don't worry about getting a perfect match – a little variation won't be noticeable.

Empty paint pots are available as part of the Citadel range should you wish to mix up large batches of paint to a specific colour.

MIXING CHART

This chart shows a series of colours that can be harmoniously intermixed or used as harmonious layers. Note that it is not necessary to use the whole series – you could pick a dark, middle and light colour out of a longer series (for example: Scab Red, Blood Red and Fiery Orange). The extreme left and right parts of each series show a colour that can be mixed to darken or lighten the series further.

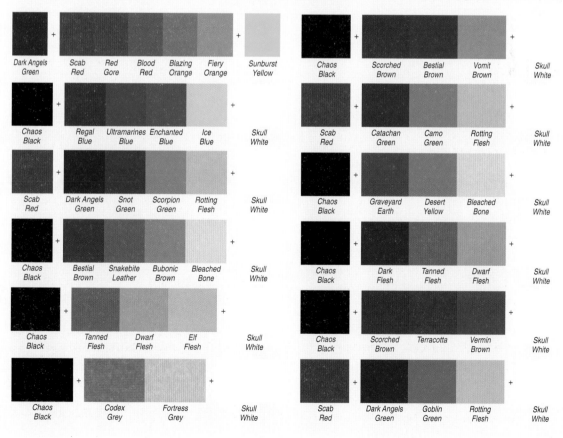

| Dark Angels Green | + | Scab Red | Red Gore | Blood Red | Blazing Orange | Fiery Orange | + | Sunburst Yellow | | Chaos Black | + | Scorched Brown | Bestial Brown | Vomit Brown | + | Skull White |

| Chaos Black | + | Regal Blue | Ultramarines Blue | Enchanted Blue | Ice Blue | + | Skull White | | Scab Red | + | Catachan Green | Camo Green | Rotting Flesh | + | Skull White |

| Scab Red | + | Dark Angels Green | Snot Green | Scorpion Green | Rotting Flesh | + | Skull White | | Chaos Black | + | Graveyard Earth | Desert Yellow | Bleached Bone | + | Skull White |

| Chaos Black | + | Bestial Brown | Snakebite Leather | Bubonic Brown | Bleached Bone | + | Skull White | | Chaos Black | + | Dark Flesh | Tanned Flesh | Dwarf Flesh | + | Skull White |

| Chaos Black | + | Tanned Flesh | Dwarf Flesh | Elf Flesh | + | Skull White | | Chaos Black | + | Scorched Brown | Terracotta | Vermin Brown | + | Skull White |

| Chaos Black | + | Codex Grey | Fortress Grey | + | Skull White | | Scab Red | + | Dark Angels Green | Goblin Green | Rotting Flesh | + | Skull White |

OPACITY OR COVERAGE

All paint is made up of a base medium and pigments and may include thickening or 'gel' agents. Many people imagine that the pigments are finely ground powders and that thick paint therefore contains a great deal of the 'good stuff'. In fact pigments are very thin liquids – the consistency of the paint comes from the medium and gel agents although the pigments can affect consistency to some extent. Whilst this has little bearing on technique as such, it helps to understand what is going on when you mix paint and when you add water and other mediums. When you mix paint, you change more than just colour – you can change opacity too. When you add water, the diluting effect can radically change the colour as well as making the paint thinner and less opaque.

Considering only acrylic paints such as Citadel Colour, it is generally the case that reds and yellows offer the least satisfactory coverage – they are the least opaque when dry. This is due to the nature of the pigments used with acrylic media.

As an experiment, try painting Blood Red (a very pure red) over a black undercoat. The result will look very brown because of the black showing through the red coat.

Now add a little white and paint this mix directly over the black. Keep adding white and comparing the results until you are familiar with the way the paint covers with different amounts of white added. You will find that the more white you add the better the coverage in one coat, which is why the more 'natural' pastel colours cover better that bright colours.

● Black Undercoat

● Blood Red

● Black Undercoat

◐ Blood Red + Skull White

● Blood Red

A practical application of this rule occurs when painting a bright red over a black undercoat. Using the 'add white' principle, first add enough white to get a completely opaque finish and cover the whole area with this.

Once the 'pinkish' colour is dry, overpaint the area with pure red, applying one or more coats depending on how solid you want the colour to be.

The same technique is good for all yellowish and pale reddish colours, such as orange and pale browns where a more 'solid' colour is desired.

This is important when it comes to painting bright reds and yellows as these colours will not completely cover over darker colours beneath, and will often look patchy when applied over white.

When it comes to making any paint cover well, there is one universal rule – add white. A red paint that is slightly pinkish will cover more effectively than a pure red or a yellowish warm red.

Colour dilution is something that varies from one colour to the next and is dependent upon the formulation of the pigment itself. The effect is most noticeable with browns. If you add water to any brown colour and paint the resultant 'wash' over a piece of white card then you will get an idea of how the colour changes with dilution. Many colours that look neutral will become yellowish or reddish when diluted. This is important when it comes to using colour 'washes', and it is well worth making up a test card as a handy reference (see the example on the right).

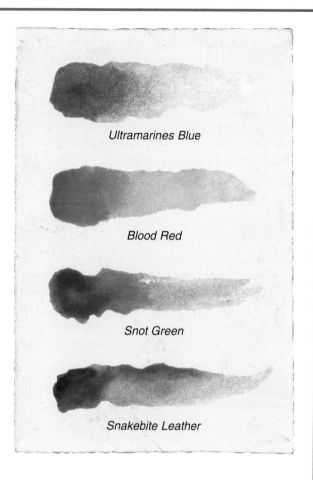

Ultramarines Blue

Blood Red

Snot Green

Snakebite Leather

OVERBRUSHING

Overbrushing is a simple and obvious way of painting highlights onto chainmail armour, hair, fur and other heavily textured surfaces. It is basically the same technique as drybrushing but instead of using a dry brush, you apply a light stroke of paint over the surface to pick out all the highlights. Many people who employ the drybrushing technique use the same word to describe overbrushing too – the two methods merge into each other and most painters will naturally combine the techniques together as they work.

The difference is that overbrushing doesn't produce the classic 'dusty' look you get from extreme drybrushing.

Mail armour is easily painted by overbrushing. Paint the mail with a dark metallic colour such as Boltgun Metal or, alternatively, mix Chainmail and Chaos Black to produce a similar dark metal colour. Then paint a lighter colour, such as Chainmail, lightly over the top so that the paint catches all the highlights on the mail but leaves the darker colour showing in all the recesses. Finally, if you want to enhance the effect, repeat with bright Mithril Silver, painting even more lightly and covering only the extreme upper surfaces of the mail.

Black undercoat

Overbrush Boltgun Metal

Overbrush Chainmail

RETOUCHING

If you find that paint is wearing from your models during use it will be necessary to periodically retouch the paintwork. This often occurs on the tips of weapons, noses and other parts that are held when the model is picked up. Models that travel a great deal will tend to wear most rapidly as some abrasion always occurs even if the models are well secured.

Because the primer coat will have rubbed away, any paint applied over the bare metal will be especially vulnerable to further wear. As these areas are exactly where the hardest wear occurs, it is worth spending a little time to make a good repair. Dot in a little white or black paint to act as an undercoat and retouch the appropriate colour as carefully as possible.

Once the repair is complete it is a good idea to apply a layer of Gloss Varnish to the area around the new paint and then respray the model with Purity Seal to remove any glossiness. The Gloss Varnish protects the paint much better than a layer of Purity Seal alone. As an alternative to Gloss Varnish, apply a layer of PVA wood glue – although white when applied, this dries to a transparent matt finish and is extremely tough.

Battle damage is a fact of life – this shows a repair to the shoulder of a Tau warrior.

STAINING

Citadel Inks are translucent colours that can be applied over a white surface, or over a black base that has already been drybrushed white, to create a colour by staining. This is similar to a wash or glaze, but both of these techniques are designed to build upon an existing colour whilst a stain provides the colour itself. Ink is ideal for this because it is highly pigmented.

Stain effects over anything other than pure white will work better for some colours than others, and it is necessary to experiment to get an idea of what the final result will look like.

This horse has been drybrushed white over black...

... then stained with a mix of Black, Chestnut and Red inks, with a little PVA glue added.

STEADY HANDS

If you have hands that are as steady as a rock, congratulations! No matter what appearance you have in mind for your models, you stand a far better chance of achieving it with a steady hand. Whilst this is undeniably obvious, there are a few methods you might find useful for keeping both subject and paintbrush steady as you paint.

Some people like to hold their model in the left hand and brace their hand against the desk top as they paint (assuming they are right-handed). This keeps the model nice and firm but means that it is necessary to stoop right over in order to see what you are doing. Painting for long in this posture is very uncomfortable and is likely to cause back or neck strain – not a good idea. If you paint in this fashion, it is best to use a low chair and try to make sure that you can see what you are doing without placing undue strain on your neck or back.

More commonly, most people will place their left elbow on the table to brace it (assuming they are right-handed) and this usually provides enough stability for all but the most detailed of work. An even more stable position can be achieved by placing both elbows on the table and resting your right hand against your left hand to lock them together. In this position both arms are braced and the work can be comfortably brought to eye level without straining either your neck or back.

Painting can become very absorbing – but it's important to take regular breaks, stretch your limbs, flex your back, walk about a bit and give your eyes the chance to relax and look at something a bit further away. Concentrating for long periods is surprisingly tiring – so it's better to paint in a series of short sessions than to blitz the job in a mammoth all-night effort. Needless to say this is all fairly obvious stuff – but there's no sight more common on the morning of a Grand Tournament than bleary-eyed competitors who have spent much of the previous night finishing their armies. Good news for the rest of us I say – at least I stand a chance if my opponent is only half awake!

Bracing your hand against the table gives stability.

Bracing your hands together allows you to bring the model closer to your eyes.

STIPPLING

Stippling is a graphic technique that is occasionally used on three-dimensional models. Basically, shades or highlights are indicated with a series of dots applied either with a pen or the tip of a brush. The density of dots defines the degree of shade or highlight. In the case of highlights, the dots can be allowed to vary slightly in size and to merge into each other, producing a pleasing dappled effect if the paint is sufficiently thin. In the case of shading, stippling works best if the dots are small and evenly sized – this is best done with a small pen rather than a brush.

Stippling used as a shading technique.

STRIPES

To paint contrasting stripes, begin with slightly dark shades of the contrasting colours. So, if painting yellow and red stripes, begin by painting stripes that are ochre and dark red. For example, add a little Snakebite Leather to Sunburst Yellow and a little Scorched Brown to Blood Red. Note that in this case similar colours are being added – both browns contain yellow and red – so the result will create a natural colour 'harmony'.

Then paint the base colours over the central part of the darker stripes leaving the contrasting edges in the original colour.

This is simply a basic layering process – in this case the darker edges tone together and mimic the visual relationship between much larger areas of colour. Anyone who has painted a wall will tell you how colours that look very pale in the paint tin can look completely overpowering when applied to a large surface – it's a similar thing at work here.

Our models are actually very small, but we want them to mimic the appearance of real life-sized objects.

If you find the layering too distinct, blend the lighter colour into the darker coat. If the subject is especially large and 'visual', such

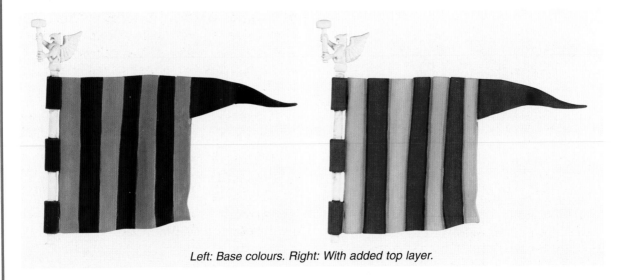

Left: Base colours. Right: With added top layer.

as a banner, this will probably be necessary. If you are just painting a model with a stripy shirt, this will not matter so much.

This is the basic method for painting stripes. Highlights can then be added either to the extreme central portions of the stripes, if they are very broad, and to areas that are naturally highlighted, such as folds.

Base colours.

With added top layer.

STUDS, RIVETS & BUTTONS

There is a very simple trick to painting buttons, studs, rivets and similar raised details where a tiny zone of hard shadow is required. Having painted the underlying colour and applied any desired shading or highlighting to the surrounding area, paint the button/stud black. Allow the paint to overlap slightly and evenly all the way round. Once this is dry, paint the button/stud in the desired colour leaving a tiny ring of very neat hard shadow round the detail. It's as easy as that.

If you wish a more subtle effect then paint the main colour for the button or stud first. When this is dry, overpaint with a suitable shade colour, allowing this to overlap slightly

● *Chaos Black*   ◉ *Burnished Gold*

more than you would with a hard shadow. Before the paint has a chance to dry, simply wipe away the shade colour from the high points with your finger – this removes most of the surrounding paint and creates a slightly smudged zone that naturally blends into the base colour beneath.

You can use the same methods to paint pus-filled boils – much beloved of Orcs, Ogres, Skaven and various Chaos models. This time use yellow as the main body colour and a red or orange as the shade colour… lovely.

You don't always have to follow the details shown on the model. Sometimes, you can add your own, as in the case of the stitching on the bandages wrapped round this model's hand.

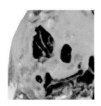
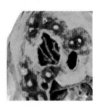

◯ *Bad Moon Yellow*   *Orange & Brown Wash*   *While wet, wipe ink off top of boils to allow yellow to show through.*

TEMPORARY MOUNTS

When painting a unit of troops, the chances are that you'll be painting a group of very similar models with the same equipment, same uniform colours, and so on.

The most efficient way of painting such a unit isn't to paint one model at a time but to work your way through the whole lot, painting all of one colour then all of another colour, and so on.

Archers fastened to a temporary card mount.

To facilitate this, it is a good idea to fix the models onto a temporary mount such as a card strip with a convenient number of models on each strip. About five or six models per strip is about right for most Warhammer or Warhammer 40,000 trooper models. This makes the process much quicker because all you need do is pick up the whole strip and apply the paint to each model along the row, turn the strip over and paint the other side, then move onto the next strip.

Of course, temporarily mounting groups of models won't suit every subject or every painter, but it is a proven method for painting whole units at a time and is highly recommended if your main reason for painting is to produce great looking armies rather than individual display models. You can use Blu-tack or similar adhesive putty to fix the models to their strip, and you can strip the models either before or after undercoating. Heavier metal models may need to be glued to the strip to hold them in place, in which case just use a light dab of superglue. The models can be separated from the card easily by slipping a knife under the bases and levering them off.

Individual models can also be fixed onto a temporary mount to make them easier to handle. In this case a piece of card might be sufficient, but most painters prefer either a cork or an old paint pot as these provide a good grip.

An old paint pot makes a useful mount.

TEST CARDS

If you mix a colour that you especially like it is well worth making up a test card showing the colours and rough proportions you have used.

Test cards are also useful ways of making a visual note about washes – simply paint the colour and then, using a little water, draw the paint into a line or squiggle to show the effect of a progressively thin coat.

The best material to use is simply a sheet of white art board or art paper – though any white paper would do, even a plain note pad.

It is worth making a few notes about proportions – it is surprising how hard it is to remember exactly what colours you used when it comes to painting a second batch of models after more than a few weeks.

THINNING PAINT

Once a pot of paint has been opened it starts to dry out and the paint becomes thicker – so its consistency varies. If the paint is a little thick, mix with water on your palette until you get a nice flowing consistency. Paint that is too thick may cover better but it will also tend to obscure fine detail – generally two thinner coats are preferable to a single thick coat.

To help prevent paint drying out in the pot, always add a little clean water to each pot after finishing a painting session. If you know you won't be painting again for a while, add more water – you can always pour off the excess if you change your mind later. It will also help if you clean away any paint from around the lip of the pot so that the lid fits snuggly. With the lid firmly replaced, invert the paint pot or give it a good shake – this deposits a thin film of paint around the inside of the lid that makes it airtight and helps prevent drying out.

If paint is too thin, firstly close the lid and give it a good shake. Sometimes the paint separates out if it has been left standing for a while and will be thicker at the bottom of the pot, so a shake or stir will even it out again. If you have added water and the top layer is very thin, pour this off first. A new pot will thicken very quickly once opened – but even more so if you leave the top off overnight!

UNDERCOAT

Retouching

You'll find that no matter how careful you are there will be some recessed areas that escape the spray undercoat. In general these areas will have a light dusting of undercoat, enough to form an effective primer, but it is a good idea to retouch them anyway. Take some paint of the appropriate colour and mix with water so that it flows readily. Now liberally paint this thinned mixture over any bits you have missed – the excess will run into the recesses. Once it has dried this will prove a perfectly adequate base colour and, in the case of black, will be sufficient for dark shading. The reason for thinning the paint is so that it will flow and completely cover the missed areas but won't form a particularly thick layer or obscure detail. Let the undercoat dry thoroughly before proceeding.

WASHES

Traditionally a 'wash' is a mix of usually strongly coloured paint and just sufficient water to give an overall fluid consistency. This mixture is applied over a light base colour and, depending on how much wash is used, will tend to run into the cracks and crevices. The result is an overall 'stain' that is stronger in the recesses where the wash gathers. This introduces a level of naturally gradated shading onto the model and breaks up the overall colour into subtle patches of dark and light. The surface finish will be slightly mottled and therefore appears more natural in the case of organic surfaces such as flesh, leather, and cloth.

The challenge with wash techniques is that the effect is very hard to control or judge. This makes it difficult to get consistently good results. A wash often looks superb when wet but the contrast diminishes as it dries. This is especially true where modern acrylic paints are used compared to some traditional mediums such as water colours and oils. To enable wash techniques to be used effectively, the Citadel Colour range includes acrylic inks that are designed to be used with washing and glazing techniques. The darker ink colours are ideal for washes, and black can be mixed in to make them even darker. Because ink contains an intense pigment in a transparent medium, it gives better results than a mix made up of paint and water.

If you wish to thin down an ink wash to reduce the intensity of colour then add water plus PVA glue. The PVA glue enhances the gathering qualities of the wash and produces a stronger contrast once dry. You will have to experiment to judge the effect for yourself. Conversely, if you want to reduce the gathering quality of an ink wash, producing a more even overall

Many people use washes for painting horses because the slightly irregular patterning of the wash gives a very realistic appearance. This is especially effective with dark coloured horses such as bays.

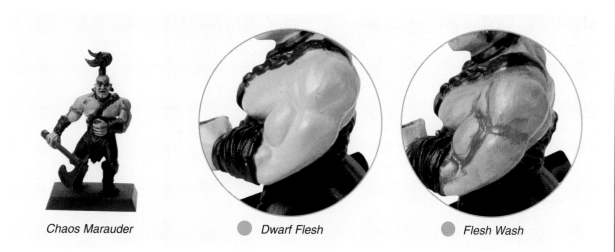

Chaos Marauder ● *Dwarf Flesh* ● *Flesh Wash*

tone, add a little liquid soap, such as washing up liquid. This breaks the surface tension so the ink stains the surface more uniformly without forming patches.

If you wish to try washing with paint, it is worth experimenting by adding Citadel Colour Varnish to the mix. This makes paint behave much more like ink and strengthens the contrast compared to paint and water alone. Again, as with all wash techniques, you will need to experiment to gauge the result. Some courage is called for!

If you use too much wash, or if the wash is settling where you do not want it, it is easy to draw away the surplus using either a brush or tissue. If bubbles form in the wash they will usually disperse quickly, but

sometimes they will dry within the recesses of the model leaving clean patches. Blowing briskly on the model will help to disperse any bubbles whilst the wash is still wet.

Washes seem to work better over pastel colours as this emphasises the contrast. Add a little white to the basecoat and observe the effect of a wash.

For the experimentally inclined, the Citadel Colour inks, paints, varnish and PVA glue can be mixed together to vary the properties of a wash. As with all techniques, improvement comes with practise, and in the case of washes it is worth performing a few tests so that you can judge the results for yourself. You can do this by taking a white undercoated figure that has a lot of flesh detail, such as a Kroot warrior, for example. Observe the different effects of using ink, dilute paint, and paint and varnish. See pages 90-91 for more details.

Kroot – large expanses of pale colour lend themselves to a wash based shading technique.

FINISHING TOUCHES

PROTECTIVE COATINGS

Purity Seal

It is usual to finish a model by applying an overall protective coating of acrylic or polyurethane varnish, or lacquer as it is also called. This serves two functions. The most obvious is to enable the models to be handled without excessively wearing or chipping the paint – this is especially important if your troops are going to see a great deal of tabletop action or are going to travel much. The other reason is to give the model an overall consistent appearance – generally to remove any unwanted shininess from inks or gloss varnish.

The usual method of applying a protective coat is to use a spray can of proprietary varnish such as the Citadel Colour Purity Seal. Similar products can be bought from model and craft shops. Car body lacquer can also be used, but note that this gives an extremely high gloss finish. Citadel Purity Seal has a semi-matt or satin finish that is very much like the natural sheen of the paint itself.

All previous comments about spraying undercoat also apply to spraying Purity Seal or other varnishes. It is especially important not to use too much varnish or the coating will run or puddle and may discolour.

A few people prefer to apply a brush-on varnish of the kind sold in DIY stores for sealing wood – these are generally polyurethane varnishes. The resulting coating is extremely tough and very shiny. You will need dedicated brushes and appropriate solvents if you want to try this method – check out the instructions on the can and make sure you have everything required including an appropriate thinner.

Most people prefer a matt or semi-matt finish to a glossy finish – but there are some who enjoy the brightness and character of gloss. A gloss finish is also tougher and does not attract dirt or dust. If you want to give models the maximum level of protection, but don't like a glossy finish, you will need to apply two coats of sealant. The first layer should be either brushed or sprayed high-gloss varnish, such as car body lacquer. This provides the maximum protection. Once this is thoroughly dry, apply a second layer in whatever finish you prefer – generally a matt or semi-matt finish such as Purity Seal.

If you want to try out any of the acrylic varnishes sold for flat artwork then make sure you test the effect first. Some matt varnishes can be far too matt if used neat and can reduce highlighting and shading effects quite dramatically. You will find that if you thin acrylic matt varnish with water it will make it less matt. You can also produce a

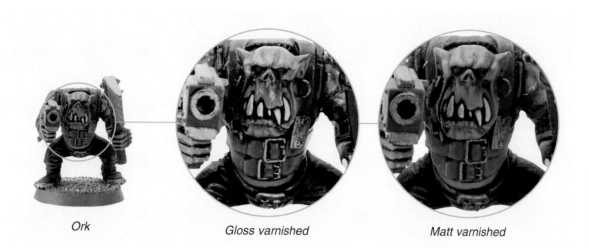

Ork Gloss varnished Matt varnished

matt finish, should you wish to do so, by painting over the surface with dilute PVA wood glue – experiment before trying this out on newly painted models.

Citadel Colour Gloss Varnish is a water-based varnish primarily intended to give gloss effects. It is not especially tough compared to polyurethane varnish. It is, however, a good way of adding a little selective protection to the points of horns, spikes, weapon tips, and other vulnerable parts of the model before applying a final coat of Purity Seal. Another way of adding extra protection is to paint a thin layer of PVA wood glue to these areas before applying the final protective coat.

GLOSS EFFECTS

Gloss Varnish

In real life, metallic, glass and some other polished objects are much more reflective than cloth, skin, wood, fur and such like. To recreate this natural shine, paint over the area with Citadel Colour Gloss Varnish. This is a water-based acrylic varnish so it can be applied in exactly the same way as Citadel Colour paint. Gloss Varnish is ideal for adding a bright gleam to sword blades or armour, gemstones, polished stones or metal, scales or slimy skin, or the inside of a monster's mouth, to give but a few examples.

Bear in mind that if you are going to apply a protective spray-on matt varnish such as Purity Seal, this will matt over the entire surface of the model. If you want a part of a model to be glossy then apply Gloss Varnish after the Purity Seal.

Gloss varnished Spawn of Chaos flesh

Gloss varnished Crossbowman armour

An army will look impressive if you take time to base the models well.

BASES

Materials

The model's base is every bit as important as the model itself and can easily make or break the finished piece. If you are painting a unit of troops or an entire army, it is by far preferable that the bases have a uniform appearance as this makes the army look coherent and purposeful. It is well worth putting a little extra effort into the bases because a painted army with expert basing will always look better than even an expertly painted army with poorly finished or inconsistent bases.

The most effective way of finishing a base is to apply a textured material – this will cover over any visible attachment points and provide an interesting ground-like surface. Suitable materials include wood or plastic decorative fillers, model railway ballast or scatter, or sand/grit or similar materials.

Wood filler and the kind of filler sold for repairing minor damage to walls are fine – they are available in pre-mixed tubs or tubes for home decorating work. Apply the filler directly to the base with a suitable modelling tool or small knife and allow it to dry. These fillers leave a smooth finish but you can introduce interesting ridges and ruts once the mix starts to stiffen. You can also press in a little grit, stones or other small features whilst the filler is wet.

Imperial Guard on snow base

Skeleton on sand base

Chaos Warrior on swamp base

An elaborate grass base

A variety of textured and pre-coloured ballast or similar scatter materials are available from hobby stores consisting of sawdust, ground up plastic, cork and such-like.

To use these, first apply a layer of PVA or wood glue to the base and then dip the base into a small heap of the material.

Try to get a good coverage and don't hesitate to re-glue and re-dip to cover any bits you might have missed.

Once dried, shake off any excess and the surface is ready to be painted. A reasonably neat if uninspired base can be produced without the need for further painting by using a self-coloured sawdust (flock).

Paint the base edge.

Apply glue.

Dip in material.

Bob's your uncle!

Keep a look out for useful materials like these.

There is an awful lot of sand in the world and much of it can be had for very little effort or cost. Sand is sold in assorted grades for building or horticultural purposes. Ordinary building or horticultural sand will endow your bases with a pleasing variety of texture – add a little fine grit to the mix if you want a few scattered rocks. This is applied to the base in exactly the same way as commercial scatter – the resultant accretion of PVA wood glue and sand is very tough. The geranium's loss is your gain.

A base texture can be applied at any time during the process but most people prefer to apply the texture either before undercoating or right at the end after the model has been painted. Most who use a black undercoat technique texture their bases before undercoating, the black provides the deepest shading on the base itself. If you use PVA glue with sand or ballast, it is important to make sure that this is dry and reasonably secure before undercoating as the undercoat may otherwise loosen the base material.

When using PVA glue and sand/ballast, you can vary the degree of texture by applying more or less PVA glue. If you use sand and find the result too 'gritty', just paint over an extra layer of PVA. The more PVA you use, the smoother the final effect will appear.

Painting Bases

If you are painting a group of models, a unit, or an army, then you will almost certainly want the bases to have a coherent uniform appearance. That means it is a good idea to choose some pre-mixed colours to use as your main colours and for the base edges. If you are going to mix up a colour, perhaps to

Here are three examples of schemes using sand textured bases over a black undercoat.

This scheme gives quite a dark base but with a lot of contrast – it suits 'evil' armies well.

Chaos Black

Overbrush
Scorched Earth

Overbrush
Bubonic Brown

Lightly overbrush
Bubonic Brown
& Skull White.

The scheme shown here gives quite a warm base colour and quite bright – add a tiny amount of green to the lightly drybrushed layers to tone down the warmth.

Dark Flesh

Overbrush
Snakebite Leather

Drybrush Snakebite
Leather & Skull White

Lightly overbrush
Skull White

This one gives a pleasing mid-toned base – the effect can be enhanced by leaving a little of the black undercoat in the deeper recesses.

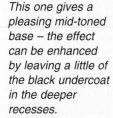
Bestial Brown

Overbrush Snakebite
Leather & Skull White

Drybrush, adding
more Skull White

use as a highlight, it is worth making up a test card so that you have a permanent record. There's nothing quite so frustrating as going back to add a new unit to an old army and not being able to match the base colours.

As with the models themselves, the textured surface can be shaded and highlighted. Novice army builders are often reluctant to apply dramatic shading to bases, but it really is surprising just how extreme you can go. The best advice is simply to find someone whose bases you especially like and shamelessly copy their scheme – most painters are only too happy to share their secrets and there is no shame in imitating the best.

But is it art?

Grass Effects

To create a covering of short fine grass use electrostatic grass – this is readily available in different shades from model railway suppliers.

The material is made of fine green fibres that mimic the appearance of grass very well. Take the base and apply PVA glue to the areas you want 'grassed'. Then dip the base into the fibres and shake away the excess. The fibres stick to the glue creating clumps of grass. The 'electrostatic' element comes from the fact that the fibres naturally acquire an electrostatic charge that makes them stand upright much like real grass. The result is very effective and, once dry, the fibres can be lightly overbrushed with a lighter colour to tone the grass back into the base.

It is possible to cover an entire base with electrostatic grass (see below) but this tends to look rather odd.

'Static' Grass base

It works better when applied in small spots over an already completed base. The strong colour and contrasting texture really helps to improve the appearance of a base that has been sand textured and painted.

Larger clumps of grass or reed can be represented by natural bristle cut from a brush, door mat, broom etc, depending on the fineness required.

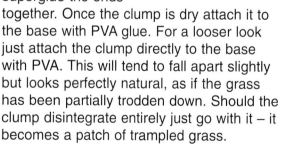

If you want the bristles to stand upright, take your clump and, keeping the ends of the bristles as tight as possible, superglue the ends together. Once the clump is dry attach it to the base with PVA glue. For a looser look just attach the clump directly to the base with PVA. This will tend to fall apart slightly but looks perfectly natural, as if the grass has been partially trodden down. Should the clump disintegrate entirely just go with it – it becomes a patch of trampled grass.

Once dry, trim with clippers to get the size and effect you want before painting the grass in your chosen colour. If the clump proves a little unstable paint on a further layer of PVA mixed with water and let this dry before painting. Grass clumps can also be anchored around small pieces of grit or gravel, or a mix of sand and PVA glue. This looks quite convincing and helps hold the bristles together whilst the PVA dries.

Here's what I call a base – not only huge but positively lathered in gruesome detail and assorted gibbly bits – you will recognise at once our man's trademark graveyard touch and doubtlessly gawp in horror at his creative use of crania. Well, maybe not – but it is very nicely done – and the use of real chunks of rock does stop the model falling over when the action gets frenzied. Just goes to show that bases contribute a lot to the finished effect – a nicely painted model based in style will always outshine a dully based model no matter how well painted.

The base of this Zombie Dragon is as much a work of art as the model itself!

TRANSFERS OR DECALS

Water slide transfers, or decals, are a great help when it comes to vehicle markings, shield designs, and designs for banners. Even if you intend to overpaint or add to a design, a transfer provides an excellent guide. A huge range of designs are available and many of these can be used in a variety of contexts and scales, so always keep a look out for useful examples.

Before applying a transfer make sure the area on the model is flat and sufficiently large to take the design and the carrier film (the clear film that surrounds the design). It is sometimes worth filing away insignificant areas of raised detail such as rivets where you intend to put a design as these will unseat the transfer and spoil the effect.

Transfers are quite fiddly to apply so it is worth having a few practice runs if you are inexperienced. You will need a saucer of water, tweezers, brush and knife. Cut out the individual design and place in the water until the transfer begins to loosen from its backing paper. Holding the backing paper with the tweezers, tease the transfer away from the backing with the brush. Once it is moving freely the transfer is ready to use.

Before sliding the transfer into place, brush some clean water over the area where you are going to put the design. Then carefully

Use a brush to tease the transfer into place.

slide the transfer from the sheet onto the model itself and slide it into position. If it starts to stick before you have properly placed it, apply more water to loosen the transfer again. Once you are satisfied with the position of the design, dab away any excess water and firm down the transfer using the brush.

If you want to blend the carrier film into the surrounding paintwork, paint around the design in an appropriate colour. If you do not want to do this then a coat of Gloss Varnish followed by a coat of Purity Seal will greatly reduce the visible line.

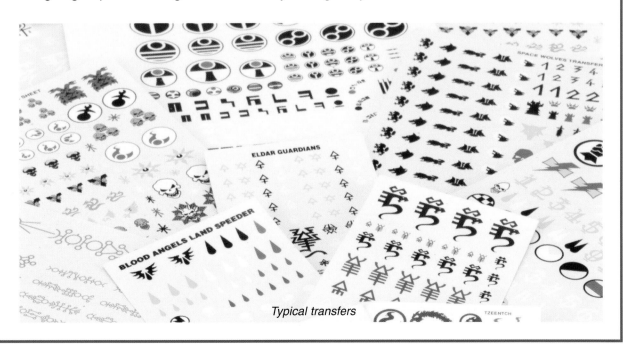

Typical transfers

Photocopy or draw out the design first.

PAINTING DESIGNS

Many people find it hard to paint shield designs, banner designs, vehicle emblems or badges, and this is one area where it really comes down to your natural talent as an artist. Even so, it is easier to copy an existing design than to work out your own, and in any case you may want to replicate one of the designs of the Warhammer or Warhammer 40,000 worlds. There are so many suitable subjects that it would be impossible to cover even a few of them here, so instead readers are directed to the individual Warhammer Armies books and Warhammer 40,000 Codexes for their source material. Here we shall restrict ourselves to the technical aspects of rending two-dimensional design.

It is always best to begin by drawing out or photocopying your design onto paper so you know exactly what you'll be doing before you begin to paint. Once you are happy with the design itself it is a good idea to photocopy it down to the actual finished size if you can do so – this gives you a better idea of how the detail will work on the model.

Begin by outlining the design onto the model using a finely tipped brush and a thin wash of paint – you can use black or sepia if the surface is light, white or grey if the surface is very dark. This outline does not need to be absolutely accurate, but you do need to get the shape and proportions right – the edges can be neatened up later. Some people prefer a sharp, hard pencil for outlining as it is easier to correct if you make a mistake. A pencil or pen is much better for large flat areas such as banners, or for large designs on the flat armoured plates of tanks.

Once you are happy with the outline, block out the basic shape in black, or in grey or white if the underlying colour is either black or very dark. When dry, apply the basic colours leaving the outline as a fine dividing line to define the image. This is not generally necessary if the background colour is black, but if the design colour is very dark then you will need a fine line of grey/white to define the shape.

In general, colours can be highlighted using a lighter shade in the centre of the area in the same way as described for painting stripes. Where areas of colour adjoin each other, it usually works best if the colours are strong or shaded where they join and lighter further away. Look at examples you like and copy the technique.

Mark out the shield design before painting.

Orc Shield

Bretonnian Shield

Skaven Shield

Undead Shield

Beastman Shield

Dwarf Shield

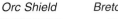
Orc Banner

Banner of Nurgle

To neaten up the outline you will need to 'cut-in' using the background colour. It is far easier to paint from the background colour and cut-in the defining line than it is to paint a perfect outline in the first place. You will also find that using a slightly darker shade of the background colour and blending or layering it back to the original colour will help to anchor the design in place – the shading stops the design looking as if it is 'floating' on the surface. If the design is dark against a light or bright colour you may need to neaten up using a white undercoat before applying the correct colour. Remember, white covers better than any other colour so is best for this kind of work.

Painting complex subjects such as pictures of monsters, heraldic creatures, daemonic heads and such like is only a question of copying the originals as faithfully as you can. As these mostly appear on banners, it is easier to paint the whole banner before fixing it to the model – and you can always practice a few times first.

If you have access to a colour photocopier and a copy of the appropriate Warhammer Armies book or Warhammer 40,000 Codex then the easiest way to make flags, banners and standards is to simply reproduce the designs at the appropriate size. If you want to personalise the design slightly then paint over or enhance the copy as required – it's much easier than starting from scratch. Photocopies can look like photocopies because they tend to be shiny. To avoid this, begin by selectively shading and highlighting the design to accentuate the banner's folds. Then apply a coat of Purity Seal to cover over the difference in texture between paint and photocopy.

Black Templars

Salamanders

White Scars

Ultramarines Banner

Ultramarines

Raptors

Silver Skulls

Dark Angels Banner

STAGE BY STAGE

This section introduces twelve stage by stage examples in a varied style by different artists. These demonstrate how the various techniques already described can be applied in a number of ways and will prove useful to anyone wishing to develop or explore their own.

Rider of Rohan
by Dave Cross

Blood Angel
by Ted Williams

High Elf Phoenix Guard
by David Imrie

Eldar Dire Avenger
by Tammy Haye

Marauder of Chaos
by Ben Jefferson

Valhallan Imperial Guard
by Dave Taylor

Dark Elf Black Guard
by Joe Sleboda

Orc
by Rick Priestley

Empire Spearman
by Dave Andrews

Kroot
by Simon Tift

Dwarf Slayer
by Nik Cristofoli

Witch Elf
by John Cadice

RIDER OF ROHAN

Dave Cross painted these Riders of Rohan using a combination of flat colours and ink washes to produce a very naturalistic effect. This demonstrates how much apparently subtle shading can be created using straightforward wash techniques. Notice how the overall shading wash not only shades the underlying colours but also imposes a uniform weathered appearance on the whole model. The style is particularly appropriate for the realistically sculpted The Lord of The Rings range as the resulting colours have a natural feel that suits the subject.

The model is painted off a black undercoat and the rider, horse, and shield are painted separately and fastened together afterwards.

1

Paint all metal areas Chainmail – scale armour painted by drawing the tip of the brush downwards to pick out detail, leaving a good amount of black below and around each scale.

2

Paint the cloak Goblin Green.

3

Paint the remaining armour Scab Red – helmet, arms, and legs.

4

Paint the clothing, saddle, quiver, and straps Dark Earth.

5

Paint the bags Bubonic Brown.

6

Apply a green shading wash to the green cloak. This is a dilute mix of Dark Green Ink, Scorched Brown paint, and PVA glue. Allow this to dry thoroughly.

7

Apply an overall brown shading wash to the whole model apart from the cloak. This is a dilute mix of Brown Ink with a little Blood Red and Chaos Black paints plus PVA glue. Allow this to dry as before.

8

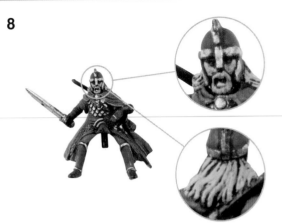

Paint the skin Bronzed Flesh and the hair Bubonic Brown leaving enough black undercoat to define the different areas and provide shading in the hair.

9

Apply a flesh coloured shading wash to the flesh and hair. This is a dilute mix of Flesh Wash with a little Scorched Brown paint and PVA glue.

10

Paint the bow Terracotta and overbrush a layer of Bubonic Brown over the grip.

11

Paint the background of the shield Goblin Green.

12

Paint the shield design Bubonic Brown leaving enough black to outline the design.

13

Apply a brown shading wash.

14

Paint the horse skin Dark Flesh.

15

Paint the saddle cloth Goblin Green and the metal details in Chainmail.

16

Apply the green shading wash to the saddlecloth and allow to dry.

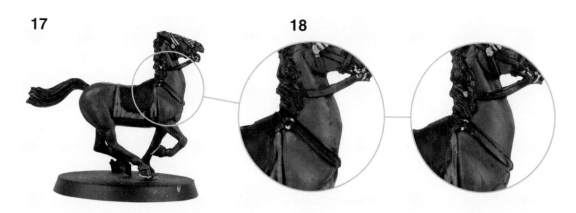

17

18

Wash the rest of the horse using the same brown shading wash but without the Blood Red.

Paint the reins, saddle and the horse's mane and tail Chaos Black.

This is one of those extremely cost effective styles that is much easier and quicker than the result might suggest. Many people shy away from wash techniques because they find the results inconsistent – the secret is really in the mix.

All the mixes used here are very dilute – the final mix should flow easily into the creases in your fingerprint when you put a drop on the end of your finger.

Gauging the consistency does take some practise – but once you get a feel for how the material behaves you can work very quickly.

Because you need to let each wash stage dry it is a technique suited to production line painting – with 10, 15, 20 or more models on the go at once. That way the first model is pretty much dry by the time you have worked through the rest of the batch.

Riders of Rohan

SPACE MARINE

I t hardly seemed possible to produce a painting guide without including at least one stage by stage example for a Space Marine – and this example Blood Angel comes courtesy of the prolific Ted Williams.

It's true that the flat plate structures on Space Marines do lend themselves to painstaking blending – but this is a time consuming process and more generally applied to individual display pieces rather than whole armies. This stage by stage cleverly gives the appearance of blending but uses shading washes and layered highlights that are much quicker and extremely effective when viewed as an army.

The model is painted off a white undercoat. It's worth noting that the boltgun has been left off until half way through as this makes the body easier to paint.

1

Paint the entire model Blood Red – don't worry if this appears patchy as the following stage will sort this out.

2

Wash the entire model with a 1:1 mix of Chestnut and Red inks to create shading.

3

Paint armour edge bands, chest eagle, pipes, eye and ear-pieces, backpack vents, armour in-fills and divisions between armour plates Chaos Black.

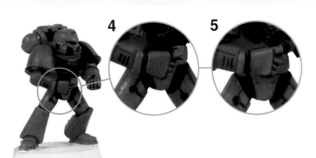

4   **5**

6   **7**

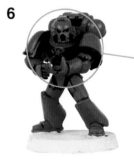 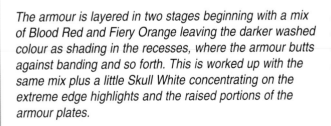

The armour is layered in two stages beginning with a mix of Blood Red and Fiery Orange leaving the darker washed colour as shading in the recesses, where the armour butts against banding and so forth. This is worked up with the same mix plus a little Skull White concentrating on the extreme edge highlights and the raised portions of the armour plates.

Paint the shoulder pad bands dark grey (mix black and white) leaving black around the edges for definition.

Overpaint the black detailing around the leg joints and on the chest eagle with the same dark grey .

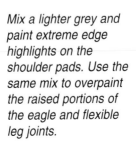

Mix a lighter grey and paint extreme edge highlights on the shoulder pads. Use the same mix to overpaint the raised portions of the eagle and flexible leg joints.

8

Paint the skull insert on the backpack Bestial Brown and layer over Skull White.

Paint metal details of armour Boltgun Metal – helmet tubing, leg plate details, earpieces & backpack vents.

9

Paint the eyepieces Dark Angels Green.

10

Paint eye piece Snot Green leaving a little of the darker colour to give a sense of depth.

11

The eyes and targeter lens get a dot of Skull White to represent reflection.

12

Paint the bolter Chaos Black and fasten to the model. The boltgun is painted in one go – paint the metal areas Boltgun Metal and layer over Mithril Silver. Paint the eagle and extreme upper edge highlight of the bolter Shining Gold. Paint the boltgun targeter lens Blood Red.

13

Apply the transfers – no shading or highlighting has been added to the transfers.

The completed Blood Angels paint scheme is admirably complemented by a dark base which sets off the strong red colour very well. This is undoubtedly a very practical way of painting a reasonably sized Blood Angels force – the ink wash provides a good shading layer from which the red colour can be worked up as you wish. Ted's preference is for a fairly strong but not overly bright red that is very convincing and gives the unit a solid, purposeful appearance.

Blood Angels Space Marines

HIGH ELF

Here's a very good example by David Imrie showing how dramatic contrasts can be used to give a very distinctive look. This is especially apparent in the flesh tones of this High Elf Phoenix Guard with show marked divisions of the fingers and areas of the face. The technique is really no different than the layering processes described elsewhere – but the colours used have been chosen to give dramatic contrasts rather than natural harmonies.

The model has been painted off a black undercoat and the base has been painted along with the rest of the model – but we shall concentrate our attention on the model itself.

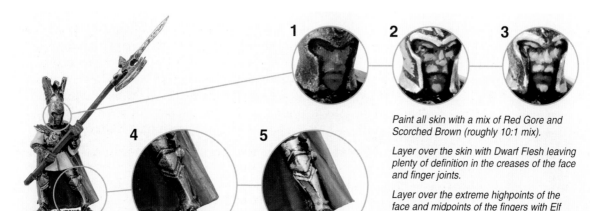

1 **2** **3**

Paint all skin with a mix of Red Gore and Scorched Brown (roughly 10:1 mix).

Layer over the skin with Dwarf Flesh leaving plenty of definition in the creases of the face and finger joints.

Layer over the extreme highpoints of the face and midpoints of the fingers with Elf Flesh.

4 **5**

Drybrush all the metal areas Boltgun Metal – don't worry about drybrushing adjoining areas as these get painted over next.

Layer over all metal areas Mithril Silver ensuring there is enough base coat left to define the detail of the armour.

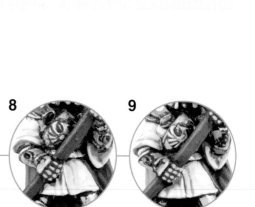

6 **7** **8** **9**

Paint the tunic Codex Grey.

Paint the halberd shaft Scorched Brown.

Layer over the tunic with a mix of Codex Grey and Skull White leaving only the deepest recesses.

Layer over raised portions of tunic with Skull White.

Layer over the halberd shaft with Bestial Brown – leave the base colour at the ends and around the hands.

Layer over the halberd shaft with Snakebite Leather leaving Bestial Brown at each end.

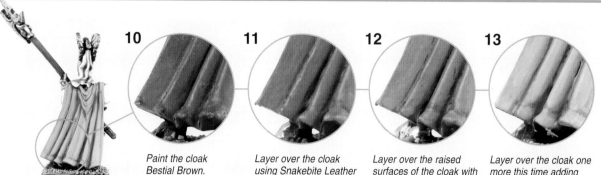

10

Paint the cloak Bestial Brown.

11

Layer over the cloak using Snakebite Leather leaving the basecoat in the deepest recesses.

12

Layer over the raised surfaces of the cloak with a mix of Snakebite Leather and Bleached Bone (roughly 4:1 mix).

13

Layer over the cloak one more this time adding more Bleached Bone to the mix. This layer on the cloak is one more than on the rest of the model – but it's worth it for the sake of all those folds.

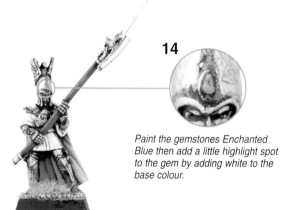

14

Paint the gemstones Enchanted Blue then add a little highlight spot to the gem by adding white to the base colour.

The final result is a very pleasing model with excellent definition. The colours used are rather subtle and it's all too easy for this to give a bland appearance to a unit. In this case the strong definition of the model's form and bold use of quite large areas of white and brown work beautifully.

Whether you like the strong contrasts on the skin or not you can't help admiring the artistry – it's a matter of taste after all – but this example shows the result very well indeed.

High Elf Phoenix Guard

ELDAR

Here we have the classic 'Eavy Metal paint job broken down into a series of stages by Tammy Haye. This is a highly popular style that photographs exceptionally well. Take a close look and you'll agree it's hardly surprising that this painstaking approach now sets the standard for competition painting and discriminating collectors.

The key characteristics of the 'Eavy Metal style are extensive use of blending, precise brush control, and time… lots of time. Preparing these stages alone took over 100 working hours. Needless to say, this isn't really a practical way of painting an entire army, but it demonstrates what it takes to produce the ultimate 'Eavy Metal style.

1

Working from a black undercoat apply a basecoat of Regal Blue to all the areas that will be finished in blue.

2

Enchanted Blue is blended over the top of the Regal Blue leaving progressively darker colour in the recesses and solid Regal Blue in the incised lines.

3

A mix of Enchanted Blue and Skull White is blended over the existing blue, taking care to work the highlights towards the edges of the individual plates.

4

The final blue highlighting is the same mix as before with added white. This time the colour picks out the edges of the plates forming an extreme edge highlight.

5

6

The helmet crest is drybrushed in two separate stages – first with a mix of Codex Grey and Chaos Black and finally with Codex Grey.

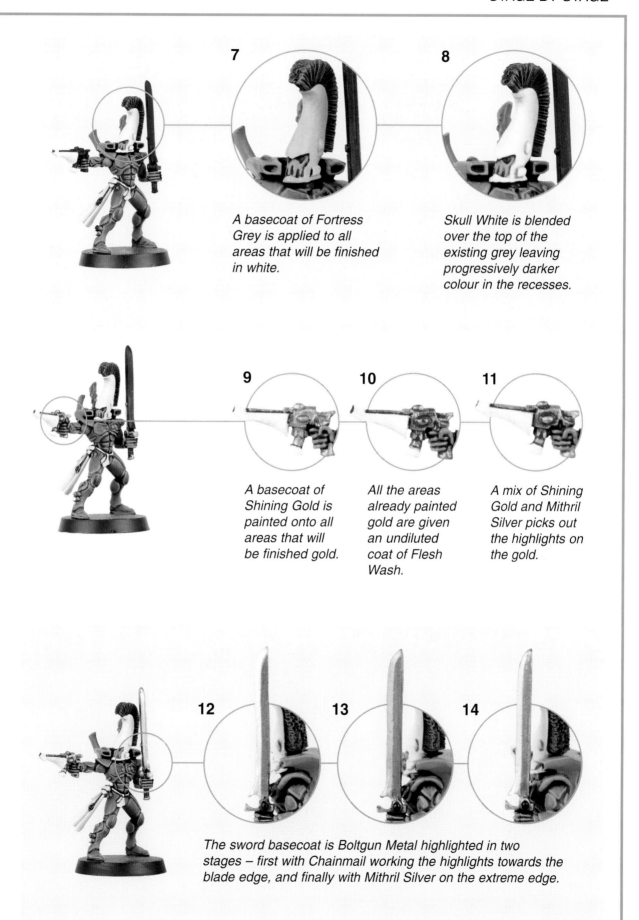

7

A basecoat of Fortress Grey is applied to all areas that will be finished in white.

8

Skull White is blended over the top of the existing grey leaving progressively darker colour in the recesses.

9

A basecoat of Shining Gold is painted onto all areas that will be finished gold.

10

All the areas already painted gold are given an undiluted coat of Flesh Wash.

11

A mix of Shining Gold and Mithril Silver picks out the highlights on the gold.

12

13

14

The sword basecoat is Boltgun Metal highlighted in two stages – first with Chainmail working the highlights towards the blade edge, and finally with Mithril Silver on the extreme edge.

All the gems are painted in four stages.

15

The basecoat is Red Gore, but the coloured area is emphasised towards the bottom part of the gem. This helps give the gem its sense of depth.

16

Blood Red is blended into the basecoat with the highlight strongest towards the bottom of the gem.

17

A fine line of Fiery Orange forms an extreme highlight along the bottom edge of the gem.

18

Finally, a small dot of Skull White is added to the top right-hand part of each gem to represent reflection.

19

The Dire Avenger sign is painted onto the helmet, and an ornamental band onto the sash, both in Regal Blue.

But would you dare play with it? Perhaps not, but that's not really the point – work like this is meant to be displayed and admired rather than subjected to the knockabout world of the tabletop wargame. A protective coating will help to preserve all that time and patience. We asked Tammy whether she'd been especially neat to make the process easier to follow. Apparently not; this is how Tammy always paints – extreme neatness is faster in the long run apparently!

Eldar Dire Avengers

MARAUDER

This Chaos Marauder painted by Ben Jefferson shows how a dramatic layering technique can produce results every bit as striking as a fully blended model when expertly applied. This example is especially useful as it allows us to see the technique at work on flesh, as well as upon cloth and wood which are more commonly painted in this way.

The model was worked up from a black undercoat and the shield was painted separately.

1

Paint all skin Tanned Flesh – don't worry about splashing onto adjacent areas as these are tidied later.

2

Layer Dwarf Flesh in bold strokes leaving plenty of definition in the recesses and upon the muscle surfaces.

3

Layer a mix of Dwarf Flesh + Elf Flesh to create highlights using bold strokes as before.

4

Paint Chaos Black to cover up any colour on non-flesh areas. This is a tidy-up stage but it also reintroduces definition around the face, belts, and so forth, so it is important to take care.

5

Paint weapon handle and fur areas in Bestial Brown, the trousers and left arm bracer in Scorched Brown and the loincloth, chest straps, leg bindings and weapon binding in Graveyard Earth. Leave enough black to divide each area.

6

7

All the brown areas are layered up in one, two or, in the case of the axe haft, three stages using increasingly fine brush strokes to create a distinct striping effect. This is especially visible on the axe haft.

These swatches show the colours used:

| Scorched Brown | Bestial Brown | Vomit Brown | 1:1 mix of Vomit Brown / Bleached Bone | Graveyard Earth | Mix of 1:2 Bleached Bone/ Graveyard Earth | Mix of 2:1 Bleached Bone/ Graveyard Earth |

8

9

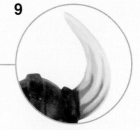

10

Paint the horns, neck torque and the edges of the boots Codex Grey. Repaint the studs on the axe haft Chaos Black and at the same time tidy where necessary.

Layer Fortress Grey onto the Codex Grey – use single strokes to create a series of distinct stripes on the horns. Add a layer of Skull White onto the tips of the horns in the same way.

Paint the eyes at the same time.

11

The metal areas are finished like either steel or brass.

The steel is Boltgun Metal with a layer of Chainmail, then washed with dilute Blue Ink, and finally Mithril Silver as an extreme highlight.

The brass is Brazen Brass with a layer of Burnished Gold, then washed with dilute Chestnut Ink, and finally Mithril Silver as an extreme highlight.

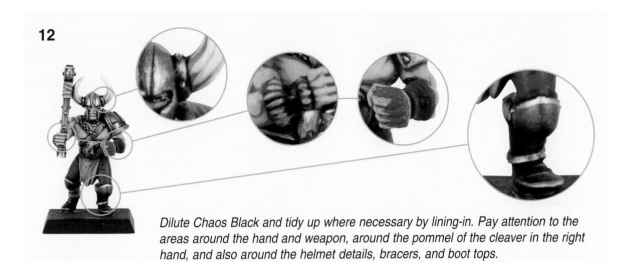

12

Dilute Chaos Black and tidy up where necessary by lining-in. Pay attention to the areas around the hand and weapon, around the pommel of the cleaver in the right hand, and also around the helmet details, bracers, and boot tops.

13

Paint the wood from a base of Bestial Brown and layer highlights.

14

Paint the shield Regal Blue and layer over a 1:1 mix of Regal Blue/Ice Blue. The extreme highlight is Ice Blue applied to the edges.

15

Paint the metal brass as for the main model.

The shield is worked up from black and the reverse drybrushed using Bestial Brown before starting. Tidy each stage with Chaos Black before going onto the next.

Ben maintains that the consistency of paint is vital for the technique he uses as the strokes are applied quite boldly and you want each stroke to produce a nicely defined line.

So don't thin the paint too much or you will find the layers starting to blend together.

Another point to note here is the amount of tidying up at each stage – something that tends to be necessary with this technique because of the way the brush strokes are formed. Tidying up allows you to retain strong definition that makes this technique so attractive.

Chaos Marauders

IMPERIAL GUARD

Dave Taylor has chosen to match his subject to his method in this example – and it really goes to show how a particular approach can suit one kind of army. In this case the army is Imperial Guard and the somewhat loose style has a very military feel that is very appropriate.

The scheme is also very simple – which is not only fitting but also helps to give a very pleasing appearance to the finished army. If you're aiming to paint fast, it's important to choose a subject suited to straightforward techniques and schemes – of which this is a very good example.

The model is worked up from a black undercoat – the base has been textured before undercoating to save time later on.

1

Use a very large brush (Citadel Tank Brush) to overbrush the whole model with Scorched Brown.

2

Lightly overbrush the model using Bestial Brown – a slightly drier brush helps to create a naturally blended look.

3

Paint the baggage and bedrolls using Codex Grey.

4

Layer Fortress Grey over the Codex Grey.

5

Paint Flesh with a 1:1 mix of Bestial Brown/Dwarf Flesh leaving plenty of black to define the recesses.

6

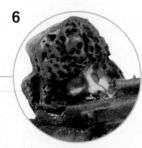

Work up the flesh with a layer of Dwarf Flesh and a final layer of Elf Flesh to pick out the highlights.

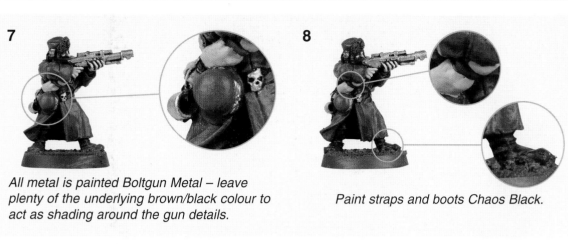

7

All metal is painted Boltgun Metal – leave plenty of the underlying brown/black colour to act as shading around the gun details.

8

Paint straps and boots Chaos Black.

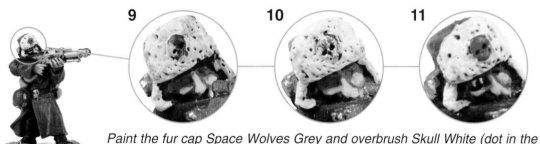

9 **10** **11**

Paint the fur cap Space Wolves Grey and overbrush Skull White (dot in the whites of the eyes while you're at it). Finally, paint the cap badge Scab Red and layer over with Blood Red.

The completed unit has been given a very nice snow effect base treatment that enhances the grim Valhallan character.

The colours work remarkably well – the underlying coat of Scorched Brown proving a uniform underpinning for the whole model. The most difficult part of this style is mastering the initial overbrushing technique. It's important to get enough colour onto the model to work as a base layer, but it's nice to get some natural blending as you would from a drybrush.

Fortunately it's a style that's easily practised and very forgiving – a solid choice for this kind of army.

A unit of Valhallan Imperial Guard.

DARK ELF

This example by veteran painter Joe Sleboda shows how several different techniques can be effectively combined on the same model – overbrushing, layering, washing and blending all play their part.

The colour scheme is interesting too – a very dramatic combination – and it gives us a chance to look in detail at a method of painting one of the most difficult colours of all – yellow!

For this example the model was undercoated white and the base texture applied and painted right at the beginning.

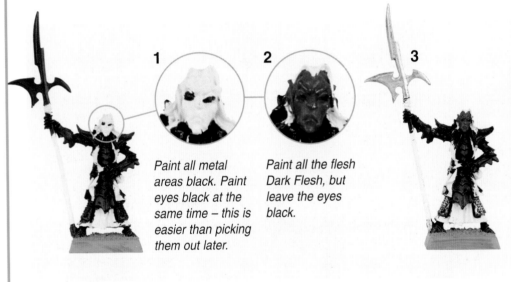

1 Paint all metal areas black. Paint eyes black at the same time – this is easier than picking them out later.

2 Paint all the flesh Dark Flesh, but leave the eyes black.

3 Paint the metal Mithril Silver. Details such as the dagger ornamentation are painted flat. Overbrush the mail to pick out the detail – this is a little messy but will get tidied later.

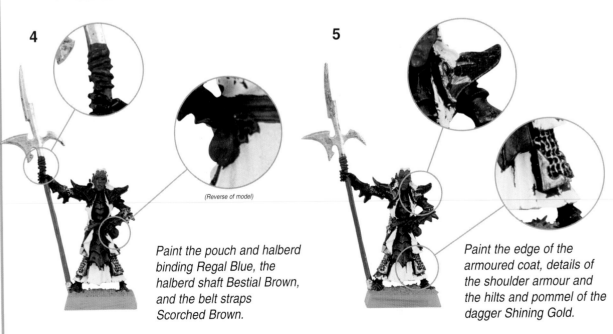

4

(Reverse of model)

Paint the pouch and halberd binding Regal Blue, the halberd shaft Bestial Brown, and the belt straps Scorched Brown.

5

Paint the edge of the armoured coat, details of the shoulder armour and the hilts and pommel of the dagger Shining Gold.

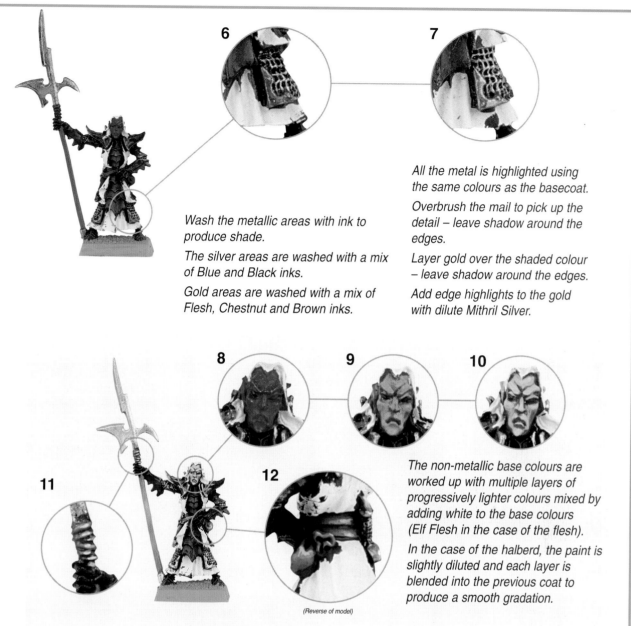

6

7

Wash the metallic areas with ink to produce shade.

The silver areas are washed with a mix of Blue and Black inks.

Gold areas are washed with a mix of Flesh, Chestnut and Brown inks.

All the metal is highlighted using the same colours as the basecoat.

Overbrush the mail to pick up the detail – leave shadow around the edges.

Layer gold over the shaded colour – leave shadow around the edges.

Add edge highlights to the gold with dilute Mithril Silver.

8

9

10

11

12

(Reverse of model)

The non-metallic base colours are worked up with multiple layers of progressively lighter colours mixed by adding white to the base colours (Elf Flesh in the case of the flesh).

In the case of the halberd, the paint is slightly diluted and each layer is blended into the previous coat to produce a smooth gradation.

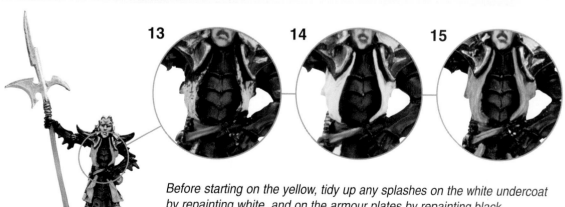

13

14

15

Before starting on the yellow, tidy up any splashes on the white undercoat by repainting white, and on the armour plates by repainting black.

The basecoat for the yellow is a mix of Red Ink, Yellow Ink, and Golden Yellow. This acts as a wash producing the dark shadow layer as a basecoat for the lighter colours, and as a guide coat emphasising the creases and folds of the cloth.

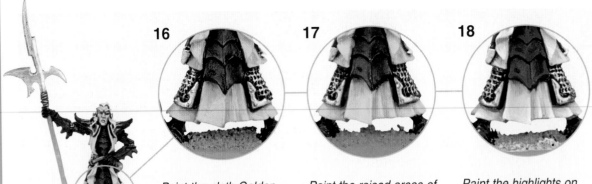

16 Paint the cloth Golden Yellow, blending the colour into the creases and folds so the deepest areas remain in the basecoat.

17 Paint the raised areas of cloth Sunburst Yellow, blending the colour into the previous coat.

18 Paint the highlights on the cloth with a dilute mix of Sunburst Yellow + Skull While, blending into the previous coat.

19 Paint the hair Chaos Black and drybrush with Chaos Black + Skull White. Finally, add dots to the corners of the eyes and highlights to the face with Elf Flesh + Skull White.

Paint an extreme highlight along the edge of the black armour plates. This was done in two stages, adding more Skull White to the Chaos Black for the second stage.

This is a striking colour scheme which provides the keynote for Joe's entire army and gives his Dark Elves a very distinct overall look. Many people find yellow hard to paint, partly because yellow paint does not cover as well as other colours. Joe actually exploits this quality by using a blending technique where the tendency of one coat to show through another is the whole aim.

Dark Elf Black Guard

84

ORC

This example, from the author, is of a very relaxed style – it's designed to be viewed from a distance so the close-up photos do tend to reveal the looseness in the technique.

Don't let this put you off – many painters find a looser style much more comfortable or faster – and the overall effect is pleasing en masse.

These Orcs are unusual in that the skin colour is not bright green but deliberately muted. This has been achieved by using a red base coat to introduce some warmth into the flesh tone, and a highly textured highlight to break up the skin surface. To make the process more visible, quite extreme colours have been used for the flesh base, flesh and highlights – but these can be varied to taste.

The whole model was painted using a large brush, applying details with the tip and splaying the end out into a chisel shape to paint the highlights.

1

Working from a black undercoat, paint the base skin Scab Red.

2

The skin is a mix of Goblin Green + Chaos Black + Skull White. Leave the Scab Red as a shade around the mouth, eyes, creases, muscles, etc.

3

Flesh highlights are Skull White plus a touch of Blood Red applied dilute with the flattened end of the brush. Lightly 'stripe' the surface of the arms and legs to create a broken 'gnarly' texture.

4

Paint the jerkin Snakebite Leather + Chaos Black + Skull White leaving the undercoat in the recesses to provide contrast.

5

Highlight the jerkin as for Stage 4 but with more white added. This is straightforward layering with a lighter shade.

6

The base colour for the teeth and claws is Snakebite Leather + Chaos Black + Skull White. Highlight colour is the same with more white added. Eyes get a dot of highlight colour.

7

All the metal detail is the same mix of Mithril Silver + Chaos Black. Leave the undercoat in the recesses and around the armour plates to give definition.

8

Bag, boots and belt were painted the same colour at the same time: a mix of Bestial Brown + Chaos Black + Skull White.

9

Highlight bag, boots and belt as before but with more white – straightforward layering once again.

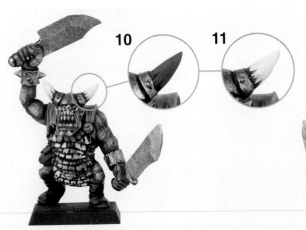

10   **11**

Bestial Brown is applied as the base horn colour by drawing the flat of the brush from base to tip to encourage a striping effect.

Snakebite Leather + Skull White is applied as the base colour for the horns, leaving a collar of Bestial Brown.

12

With a wash of Chaos Black + Bestial Brown define the area around the arms, the lacing on the tunic, the deep creases in the tunic and around the belt. This neatens up the folds and creases and helps to disguise the large flat area where the jerkin hangs from the arms.

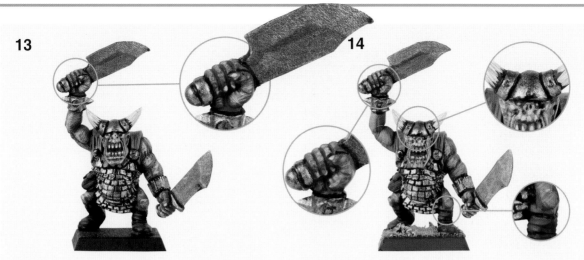

13

With a wash of Chaos Black + Bestial Brown, paint over the weapon blades and wipe away excess, leaving a stain. This helps break up the large flat surface of the blades by introducing a texture.

14

Dilute Chaos Black and tidy up where necessary by lining-in. Pay attention to the areas around the hand and weapon, around the pommel of the cleaver in the right hand, and also around the helmet details, bracers, and boot tops.

As a unit some variation is introduced by using slightly different colours or varying the mixes from one model to the next. The Scab Red base works well around the eyes and mouth but a darker base coat might provide better definition around the muscles – try adding a little Dark Flesh to the Scab Red. The highlights are pretty extreme (I wanted them to show up in the photos) but I have to say I rather enjoy the effect! A less extreme version would be to add Goblin Green to the mix.

Orc Warriors

EMPIRE SPEARMAN

This example ably demonstrates how effective a basic layering technique can be. These stages have been put together by Dave Andrews who is an enthusiastic exponent of this method as well as a keen wargamer whose superb public demonstration games have won many awards and much praise.

The technique is well suited to producing attractive armies quickly and many would regard it as setting the standard for army painting. The important thing with this layering style is to be neat and Dave's exacting brush control serves him very well as you can see.

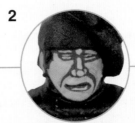

1

Working from a black undercoat, paint a base coat of Dark Flesh to the flesh areas.

2

Layer over a mid-tone of Dwarf Flesh leaving the dark colour in the shadows and creases to emphasise the facial features.

3

Layer over highlights of Elf Flesh to the raised parts of the face, in particular the nose, cheeks, chin and forehead.

4

5

6

7

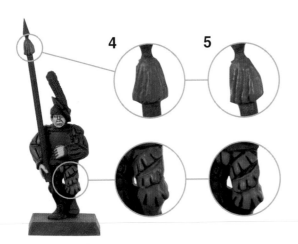

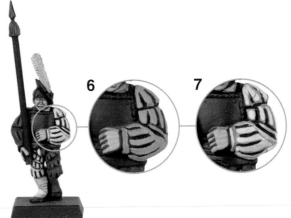

Paint the red clothing and spear tassel Scab Red.

Layer the Scab Red over the folds in the cloth so that the black undercoat is left in the slashing and deepest creases.

Layer over Blood Red to create highlights.

Paint the white clothing and plume Fortress Grey.

Layer the Fortress Grey over the folds in the cloth in the same way as for the red.

Layer over Skull White to create highlights – the plume is lightly overpainted to pick out the detail.

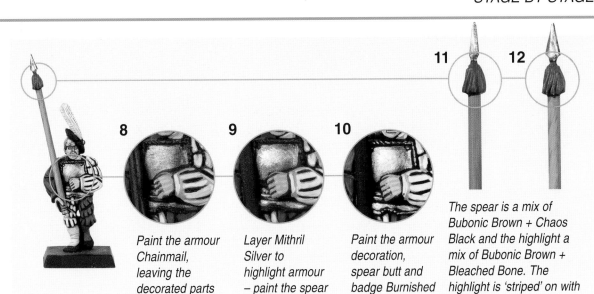

8 Paint the armour Chainmail, leaving the decorated parts black.

9 Layer Mithril Silver to highlight armour – paint the spear tip at the same time.

10 Paint the armour decoration, spear butt and badge Burnished Gold.

11 **12** The spear is a mix of Bubonic Brown + Chaos Black and the highlight a mix of Bubonic Brown + Bleached Bone. The highlight is 'striped' on with a large brush to create a wood-grain effect.

13 **14**

The shield is painted separately, working off a black undercoat. Paint the device and rim Brazen Brass leaving black in the recesses. Highlight with a layer of Burnished Gold.

The interesting thing about this example is how the absolute minimum of layers have been used to achieve the final result: three layers over black for the face and only two layers over the clothing (the hat is left undercoated black). Although Dave will often happily apply multiple layers where the effect is worthwhile, he generally advocates two as sufficient for most purposes. By using the minimum of layers, the effect is solid and unfussy. To give you some idea of comparative speeds, these stagers took about five hours to prepare.

Empire Spearmen

KROOT

Simon Tift is the owner of an extremely attractive Kroot army painted with a combination of techniques – wash, drybrushing and blending.

Simon is particularly adept at using washes – see his comments at the end – and this works especially well with the pastel coloured skin colour of the Kroot.

The model is painted over a white undercoat.

1

2

Paint the skin Rotting Flesh. Next, apply a shading wash to the skin. This is a mix of 1 part Black Ink, 1 part Brown Ink, 10 parts Green Ink, 10 parts PVA glue, plus about 20 parts water (ie, roughly half water).

3

4

Paint the straps, armour pads and the beak and belly of the Kroot Snakebite Leather.

Apply a shading wash over straps and armour pad. This is a mix of 1 part Brown Ink, 1 part Black Ink, 1 part PVA glue, plus about 3 parts water (ie, roughly half water as before).

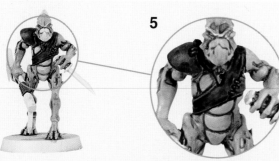

5

6

Blend Bleached Bone over the beak and belly of the Kroot. Add Skull White to the Bleached Bone and blend this over the previous coat.

Add more white and continue blending until the final highlight is almost white.

7

8

9

Paint the weapons and the Kroot's crest black.

Carefully drybrush a mix of Tin Bitz and Boltgun Metal over the black areas on the gun and knife handle.

Apply a metal stain over the metal areas. This is a mix of 1 part Black Ink, 1 part Brown Ink, 2 parts water plus a little washing up liquid.

Once this is dry, highlight the weapons by carefully drybrushing with a mix of Brazen Brass and Dwarf Bronze.

10

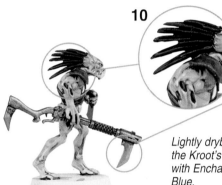

11

12

13

Lightly drybrush the Kroot's crest with Enchanted Blue.

Paint knife blades Chainmail, leaving plenty of shadow to define where the blades attach to the gun and hilt.

Apply the metal stain over the blades as before.

Paint the details Burnished Gold.

Apply the same metal stain as before.

The whole effect comes from contrasts produced by the skilful use of washes both to shade and to stain. The shading washes include PVA glue – this makes the wash viscous and encourages the pigment to gather in the folds and hollows without 'puddling'. The wash used as a metal stain includes washing up liquid which reduces the viscosity of the wash, allowing it to run more freely over the whole surface. Simon used the same shading wash over a variety of base colours for the entire army, providing a contrast between the Kroots and Krootox, for example, without having to formulate a different wash for each. By adding a little Dark Angels Green and Chaos Black to the base colour of the Krootox, the overall appearance becomes quite distinct.

Kroot

SLAYER

This Slayer, painted by the prolific Nik Cristofoli, provides us with a fine example of how to get the most out of a black undercoat for a practical and speedy style with good definition and colour.

As with most Dwarf models much of the character of this piece comes from the beard, and it is easy to see the excellent depth of shading derived from the use of the black undercoat and colour washes. Notice also how a good width of black has been left at each stage to define areas such as the axe blade, hair and axe shaft – this requires care but saves time later redefining areas by lining-in.

The model was prepared and given a black undercoat prior to painting.

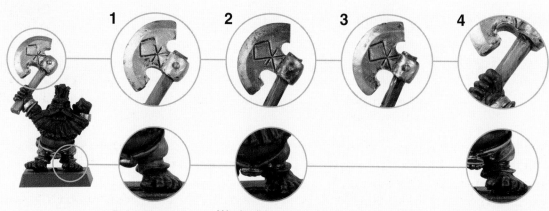

1 Paint all metal parts Boltgun Metal and paint the axe shaft and trousers Bestial Brown.

2 Wash all brown and metal parts with a mix of Brown and Black inks.

3 Layer all metal parts Chainmail, leaving shading in recessed and shadowed areas.

4 Layer axe haft and trousers with a mix of Skull White and Bestial Brown, leaving shading around edges and in recessed areas.

Overbrush all hair Skull White to serve as an undercoat.

5 Overbrush the hair Golden Yellow.

6 Wash the hair with Orange Ink.

7 Drybrush the beard with Sunburst Yellow, working up highlights with a mix of Sunburst Yellow + Skull White.

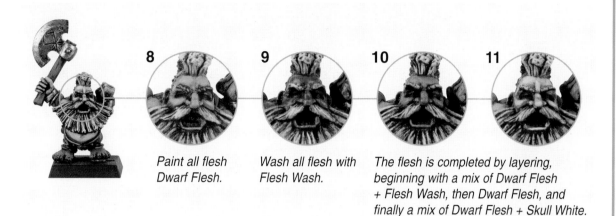

8 Paint all flesh Dwarf Flesh.

9 Wash all flesh with Flesh Wash.

10 The flesh is completed by layering, beginning with a mix of Dwarf Flesh + Flesh Wash, then Dwarf Flesh, and finally a mix of Dwarf Flesh + Skull White.

11

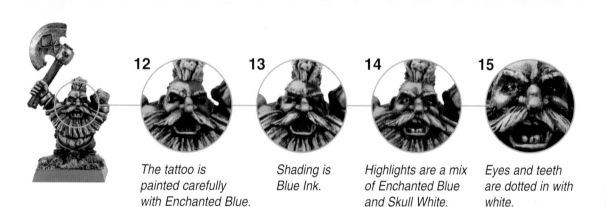

12 The tattoo is painted carefully with Enchanted Blue.

13 Shading is Blue Ink.

14 Highlights are a mix of Enchanted Blue and Skull White.

15 Eyes and teeth are dotted in with white.

Overall the result is a very pleasing model with a great deal of visual depth to it. A lot of the effect comes from the black undercoat but careful use of washes also contributes by adding shade and richness.

In this example the yellow beard also gives us another chance to see that painting yellow over black need not be a problem so long as you selectively undercoat in white first.

Slayers

WITCH ELF

It's not everbody that would think of painting a skin tone over blue, but here it works very nicely, lending a hard-edged, cadaverous beauty to these gorgeous Witch Elves. John Cadice's approach is to paint rapidly with slightly dilute colours, allowing him to combine layers with a little quickly executed blending as he goes. John claims to complete units of twenty models over a couple of evenings – and that's going some – but the result is a very stylish and appealing army nonetheless.

The model is painted from a white undercoat.

1 Paint hair, skin and clothes with a dilute wash of Storm Blue mixed 1:1 with Tentacle Pink.

2 Drybrush using a mix of the base colour with a little Skull White added.

3 Add more white to the mix and work up the hair to almost pure Skull White.

4 Paint the flesh – this is a mix of 1 part Midnight Blue and 1 part Tentacle Pink (as before) plus 2 parts Elf Flesh.

5 The flesh is finished by progressive layering of Elf Flesh and Elf Flesh mixed with Skull White.

6 The final layer is almost pure white – the colour of these fatal beauties should be pale and cold!

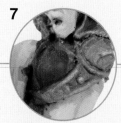

7 Paint the cloth in a 2:1 mix of Midnight Blue and Tentacle Pink.

8 Work up the colour by layering over a mix of the base colour and Skull White.

10

Paint all the metal, straps, boots, eyes and mouth black.

11

Paint the sword blades Chainmail – paint the studs at the same time.

12

Paint the remaining metal areas Dwarf Bronze.

13

Add a little of the Tentacle Pink and Midnight Blue base colour to Skull White (about 1:3) and paint extreme highlights to the edges of leather straps and boots where this helps to accentuate the shape.

14

Paint the eyes white and dot in the pupils using Warlock Purple – paint the narrow eyebrows while you're at it.

John maintains that the key is to work quickly – don't kill yourself trying to be too precise or doing too much, and pay attention to what really makes the model special. It's interesting to see how the blue mix underscores the whole model and even gets mixed into the final extreme edge highlights to reinforce the whole feel.

Witch Elves

BLANCHITSU

John Blanche

John Blanche is Games Workshop's Art Director and a pioneer in the art of painting miniatures. For many years he ran a highly acclaimed regular painting column in White Dwarf called Blanchitsu.

He has a very distinctive 'painterly' style of painting models, reminiscent of his artwork, as can be seen from the examples on this page.

Converted Mephiston, Blood Angels character

"Neutral colours are generally brownish or greyish mid-tone colours that will tend towards either the warm (red) or cold (blue) end of the spectrum. The overall appearance of an army depends very much on whether it has an overall warm or cold cast. On the whole, warm colours will give a much more pleasing appearance and some painters will make a point of using only warm colours for all subjects.

Converted Warhammer 40,000 Inquisitors

Primary colours red, blue and yellow, are best avoided except as spot colours, but can be used effectively as contrasting bands or design details applied over white or off-white. Some people feel that primary colours convey a primitive quality suggestive of Egyptian, Aztec, Sumerian or similar ancient cultures.

Red, black and white are the three most graphic colours and make excellent spot colours when applied to plumes, tassels, and similar small decorative details.

Converted 54mm scale Inquisitor.

Red carries strong military connotations for most of us – it is the colour of blood, of British red-coats, of Spartans, and of Roman legionaries. As such it works well as a theme colour for spot colours, designs, and banding."

Converted Mordheim Zealot